Voices of the Authors

"My voice has been enriched by the individuals who have offered their stories in Voices From Subsistence Marketplaces. The opportunity to get to know the men and women who battle every day to survive and to make the lives of their children better helped to burst the privileged bubble in which I live. The voices in the book have expanded my understanding of the diversity of the human experience."

-John Hedeman

"The richness, depth, and resourcefulness of the people inside this book are what struck me the most. We can all learn many lessons from them. I know I did."

-Tom Hanlon

"It gives you a window into the lives of individuals who might be living in poverty, but have rich lives in all other facets just like you and me. The emphasis is on human stories rather than generalizations about poverty. "

-Srinivas Venugopal

"Voices From Subsistence Marketplaces was created with the idea of bringing out the lives and stories of those we've met while working in different parts of the world. In a sense, our research has been about bringing out voices previously unheard. Through our interactions, we have been fortunate to meet hundreds of people, who have generously shared their lives and experiences."

-Madhu Viswanathan

1

VOICES

FROM

SUBSISTENCE

MARKETPLACES

JOHN HEDEMAN - TOM HANLON
SRINIVAS VENUGOPAL - MADHU VISWANATHAN

I0407267

Voices From Subsistence Marketplaces

By:

John Hedeman, Tom Hanlon, Srinivas Venugopal, and Madhu Viswanathan

ISBN-13: 978-1543195989

Published by Madhu Viswanathan

3

Contents

A special thanks to the women and men who allowed us to interview them and courageously shared their stories.

Preface
By Steven Morse

When we wake up, many of us have some idea as to what the day may hold. Though not everything is planned; we have a degree of control; we have backup options; and we can see some event or destination on the horizon. We have dreams, aspirations, expectations for fulfillment. If something goes wrong, we probably have a support system in place. Many people throughout the world live without these certainties and margins of error. Those living below the poverty line encounter many extreme challenges. Maybe they are sick and they must choose between eating or seeking treatment, or maybe even worse, their children get sick. Still, these individuals at the bottom feel the awe of the new day and somehow find a passion that drives them forward. They feel the broadening of their minds. They encounter great tragedy and they experience great loves that lead them to incredibly selfless actions. Those around the globe living in subsistence settings feel and interact in ways that are both wildly different, and so touchingly familiar to our being. Through the work of the Subsistence Marketplaces Initiative, University of Illinois, and the Marketplace Literacy Project[1], the authors of this book have encountered numerous, stunning individuals located in what we term subsistence marketplaces. Set within India, whether it be extreme poverty in rural South India, or in the bustling city of Chennai, this book aims to capture the voices of those whose stories, struggles, and powerful character would otherwise go untold.

Each person you will meet in this book has shared with us their lives, openly and passionately, and we are humbled by the opportunity to

---

[1] See "About The Subsistence Marketplaces Initiative" for more information.

bring them to light. We have met some of these individuals on numerous occasions, while others have come to us but once in our interviews to tell us about themselves. Many of these stories were told in the sweltering Chennai heat, amongst the rolling power blackouts that do not phase our interviewees. Some were told to us outside a small thatched hut next to sprawling rice paddies. Many individuals sacrificed their time, which meant skipping important income-generating activities of the day, to simply share their stories with us. We do our best to share these voices - these stories of sacrifices made to survive and make lives better for the next generation. These men and women are visited in areas where our affiliated non-profit partner, the Marketplace Literacy Communities (MLC), has been established, where our subsistence marketplaces research has been conducted, and where students of the University of Illinois have visited.

Our steadfast intentions and good standing in the communities we have worked with, have brought forward many remarkable individuals. Of those, there are many whom we routinely encountered, developing a larger picture as to who they were on each visit to their communities. These stories have been the accumulation of years of repeated visits.

As we navigate the space of this book, it is important to note that these voices have been captured and interpreted by four key authors: John Hedeman, Tom Hanlon, Madhu Viswanathan, and Srinivas Venugopal (of whom you can learn more about in the back of this book). Each individual capturing these stories comes from a different background and has often developed a deeper personal relationship with each of the characters who are represented on these pages.

For some, sharing their stories acts as a type of therapy; few in these settings have the opportunity to talk openly of their family and personal struggles. With what we hope was patience, understanding, and courteous intrigue, we have brought out the essence of these individuals.

As you journey through these pages, note that often we include sidebars that deviate from the story. With the vast cultural differences, background into India's cultures and norms can be enlightening as well as pivotal to your interpretations. The stories themselves are drawn from direct translations of our subjects' interviews. Further detail that brings these stories alive come from insights into the marketplace that our team has developed from many years of research, interaction, and study in these communities.

Some of these stories will also be made available online at **www.voicesfsm.com** in due course, along with further multimedia relating to the individuals on these pages. We know that you will gain great perspective and a greater appreciation for the gifts in your life from these stories, but we hope that you also develop a new appreciation for the hardships that others around the globe face every day as they struggle to meet even the most basic needs such as fetching water or obtaining basic medical care. As these resilient individuals tell their stories of poverty, struggle, brilliance, great hardship and misfortune, ingenuity, love, and bold character, we hope you take time between stories to delve further into these individuals' lives and draw parallels to your own identity. What matters most to you? Who would you make similar sacrifices for? Where do you acknowledge everyday beauty? How would you handle tragedy? By the time you finish reading this, we believe you will be more in tune with yourself and feel a newfound oneness for those without a voice. Please read on and enjoy Voices From Subsistence Marketplaces.

About The Subsistence Marketplaces Initiative[2]
And The Marketplace Literacy Educational Program

The Subsistence Marketplaces Initiative in the College of Business at the University of Illinois has pioneered a bottom-up approach to research and practice at the intersection of poverty and marketplaces. Unique to our approach is a bottom-up orientation that begins with a micro-level understanding of buyers, sellers, and subsistence marketplaces. We adopt a marketplace rather than a market orientation, viewing subsistence contexts as more than markets to sell to, rather as individuals, communities, and preexisting marketplaces to learn from. Our focus should be distinguished from macro-level economic approaches and mid-level business strategy approaches such as base-of-the-pyramid (BOP) research. Our goal is to understand and enable the progress from subsistence marketplaces to sustainable marketplaces, i.e., marketplaces characterized by sustainable production and consumption that enhance individual and community welfare and conserve natural resources.

Our efforts in research have generated more than 40 authored publications, and we have edited roughly 60 refereed publications through special issues and organized six biennial conferences bringing together scholars and practitioners. Direct educational experiences, derived from our experiences on this topic, reach almost a thousand students a year at the University of Illinois and many more students online, including a yearlong interdisciplinary course and a one-of-a-kind international immersion experience that has been ranked one of the top 10 entrepreneurship courses by Inc. Magazine. Educational materials are disseminated worldwide through a web portal. This work has led to a unique marketplace literacy educational program that tens of thousands of individuals have received in six countries – India, USA, Tanzania,

---

[2] The text is excerpted directly from websites for the Subsistence Marketplaces Initiative.

Preface

Uganda, Argentina, and Honduras – through the Marketplace Literacy Project, a non-profit organization founded in concert with this initiative and other partners. In India, we have worked with partners to deliver marketplace literacy to more than 40,000 women.

Whereas previous work has focused on at least two key elements that individuals living in subsistence need to participate in marketplaces, financial resources (e.g., microfinancing), and market access, marketplace literacy is the third key element. Research aimed at understanding life circumstances and marketplaces in subsistence contexts in urban and rural parts of South India was a basis for developing a consumer and entrepreneurial literacy educational program which assumes that the audience cannot read or write. This program uses the "know-why" or an understanding of marketplaces as a basis for the know-how of being an informed buyer or seller. Despite the difficulties with abstract thinking that low-literate individuals may experience, such education enables deeper understanding of marketplaces by leveraging the social skills that participants bring to the program and relating educational content back to their lived experiences. The program innovates in terms of the content as well as the delivery method, covering concepts using picture sorting, role plays, and so on, that tap into people's lived experiences. Such understanding can enable individuals to place themselves on a path to lifelong learning. Topics covered range from consumer skills to choosing an enterprise to start and being customer oriented and engaging in sustainable practices. The approach is documented in a book, Enabling Consumer and Entrepreneurial Literacy in Subsistence Marketplaces, published by Springer in an education series in alliance with UNESCO. Further information can be found at **www.voicesfsm.com**.

☐

10

Chapter 1

Rahamat: Reshaping Her Destiny

"It was very difficult for me to keep my children under somebody's care, but I didn't have any other way. I didn't have any male member to support my family. Till their marriage I am doing the role of both male and female."

Rahamat's destiny is turning out better than it began.

She was married at age 12 to a man twice her age. Still a child herself, she soon gave birth to two sons and two daughters. Her husband, whom she says "did not have good habits," died at age 40, when she was 27. She mourned his loss, to be sure, but she did not allow lengthy mourning, because she had four children who needed caring for. She needed to take action. What action, she didn't know. But she could not afford to sit and do nothing.

Put yourself in her shoes: 27, four children (the oldest being 11), a fifth grade education, no money to her name, no job, no one to help her, no way to raise her children.

And, she thought to herself, this is no way to raise my children. I must do something.

~~~

"Come," she says to her youngest son. "It is time to go." She stands in her one-room apartment, holding a cloth bag in each hand. Her

11

children's clothes are stuffed in both bags. Her other children are outside, waiting.

"I don't want to go," the boy whines.

"But you will be with your grandmother. Come on. We do not have time to waste."

The boy groans but dutifully gets up. She leads her four children, like a mother duck leading four ducklings on a journey, which they are all surely on. They follow her through the streets of Chennai until, a half hour or so later, they arrive at the tiny apartment where Rahamat's mother lives. Her mother can take in only one child; she takes the youngest. Rahamat leaves her youngest with her mother and takes her other three children to a hostel down the street. She has arranged for them to stay there and their grandmother will look after them.

The hostel is an old, white stone building. It has a large, open room with many beds on the sides and a kitchen and toilet in the back. The floors and walls are stained but clean. Light filters through a few small windows.

The kids warily eye the place. The two girls have tears in their eyes.

"I don't want to stay here," the youngest girl says.

"It is what you have to do for now," Rahamat says firmly. "I have a good job to go to. I will send money every month."

"Please don't go," the other daughter says. She hugs Rahamat, and Rahamat's eyes become moist.

"I have to go. It will be better for us. You will see," she says.

She wills herself to think about the children's future. She puts away her present sadness to focus on her goal of securing a good future for her children.

~~~

To secure that future, Rahamat makes a journey of nearly 4,000 kilometers, to a land she does not know, to a language she does not speak (she learned Arabic in three months, out of necessity), to customs that seem as foreign as the language to her. She has found domestic work in Ras al-Khaimah, one of the seven emirates that make up the United Arab Emirates, through friends. She makes 400 dirams per month – about $100 USD – working for an Iranian family. She sends some money home each month and puts the rest in the bank. She doesn't need much to live on herself.

Her plan, you see, is larger than survival. It is larger than just having enough to buy food, to have a roof over her children's head. If she thought that way, she would never get ahead.

But she thinks in a different way. To worry about food, about water, about rent, is not going to be her destiny, and it is not going to be her children's destiny. She is a woman of faith, and her faith helps her persevere. She recites scriptures to herself to bolster her faith and to give her confidence to move forward.

At night, she lies in her bed in the house where she works. It is a good bed, much better than any bed she has slept in. She thinks of her children sleeping in the hostel on old mattresses or on mats on the floor. She thinks of them sharing a toilet with so many people. It is not what they want, and it is not what she wants.

For a time, it has to be that way. And she is moving, slowly, inexorably, toward a day when it will not have to be that way. Her mother and her grandmother have passed on a determination to her that is born of selflessness and a desire for a brighter future for the ones she loves: her children. That is how her grandmother was toward her mother; that is how her mother was toward her. And that is how she is toward her children.

Her goal is like a distant mountain. She is moving toward it, but sometimes it seems so far away.

She pushes the thought out of her mind that her children will hate her for abandoning them, for leaving them so far away. Or worse, that they will forget her.

She tells herself to stay focused on the reason she is in Ras al-Khaimah. But sometimes it is hard to do. It is especially hard because the couple who employ her are not kind to her. They have no patience with her because she does not know the language. She doesn't understand much of what they say to her, but the scowls on their faces and the tones of their voices speak a universal language.

Still, she thinks, I must keep my back straight. My head up. I must work hard. I must send money home to my children. And I must save for their future.

~~~

She does this for three years. Along the way she becomes conversant in Arabic. She augments her language skills by reading the Koran. She puts up with the verbal abuse from the couple in exchange for money to send home. Every month she sends some money home and puts some in the bank. The weeks and months and years roll on. Her children are growing and her bank account is growing, too.

That mountain that she is walking toward is beginning to draw closer. And she is beginning to walk toward it with a bounce in her step, with confidence.

This journey has not been easy, she tells herself. But surely I will get there.

~~~

Three long years.

That is how long it has been since she has been to Chennai, indeed anywhere in her home country.

That is how long it has been since she has kissed her children, since she has made them a meal, since she has prayed over them, since she has made sure they have tended to their studies.

In other words, since she has been a mother to them.

Through a placement agency, she has found more domestic work in Riyadh, Saudi Arabia. But before she starts her new job, she journeys back home to Chennai. She needs to see her family. That is a must. Three years is an eternity.

But now, as she nears Chennai, the mountain that she has been walking toward for those three long years – securing the future of her children – looms larger than ever.

Yes, she has sacrificed much in that time. She has lost years with her children that she cannot get back. But she has also gained something. She has saved enough money to buy a house—meaning, a few rooms in an older urban building. This is not what Westerners would consider a "house," but it is understood as such in India. Rahamat's house would be considered a very meager and humble apartment in Western culture, but her children have never lived in a place they have owned. She is introducing them to a new way of life, a new way of operating in the world.

By the sweat of her brow and the will of her heart, she is giving them a hope for the future.

~~~

She spends a few months with her children and mother. She cannot believe how her children have grown. They appear to have blossomed before her very eyes. They look healthy and they are happy to see her.

Rahamat: Reshaping Her Destiny

It is joyous to be back home among people who speak her own language and follow the same customs. She sleeps deeply and peacefully at night, and her body regains energy that had been sapped through her hard work and long journey.

But as the time draws near to depart again, this time for Saudi Arabia, the familiar sadness creeps into her heart. Her eldest daughter clams up, distancing herself from Rahamat. Her youngest son acts up, drawing attention. Her other two children grow moody.

"It cannot be helped," she says on the night before she is to leave.

"You could get work here in Chennai," the younger daughter says.

"Work here is not easy to find. And it would not pay as much as I am going to make in Riyadh. If I had not gone away to work, we would not have this house."

They cannot argue that, but still the evening ends poorly, with feelings ruffled all around, and the sadness in Rahamat's heart growing heavier. Her last night in Chennai is the only night that she does not sleep well during her return home.

~~~

Rahamat spends a few years as a domestic in Riyadh. She continues to save and to send money home. The children continue to grow. They are of marrying age now. After a few years, Rahamat gets another job, through an agent, in Doha. She works in Doha for some years and then returns to Chennai, this time for good. She does so because she does not want to lose her children. She wants to get them married.

So she returns to the city where she was born, and she begins a textile business, buying and selling saris. She marries her children off; all four are married now, and all four have given her grandchildren.

She returns a changed woman. She has spent 11 years in foreign countries confronting challenges, hardships, fears, and obstacles. But those confrontations have proven successful. Because, in those 11 years, she has successfully reshaped her destiny.

She left the country penniless. She returned soon to be using her innate entrepreneurship skills, to help herself and the community around her, although she perhaps did not know it at the time.

She left India filled with doubts and fears. She returned filled with confidence and hope.

She left from a position of weakness. She returned from a position of relative strength.

"The separation was very hard," she acknowledges. "I did not want to leave my children. But I knew to truly help them, I must leave. I had to be both mother and father to them."

Rahamat has not only helped her own children; she has helped many young women who are in the same position she was in many years ago. She leads a women's self-help group in Chennai, and she is a mother figure to many of the younger members of the group.

"My primary goal with my group is to help these women grow in self-confidence," she says. "I want to help them develop a fighting spirit. Women have to fight. They have to have courage."

~~~

Rahamat is a natural entrepreneur with a fierce drive to earn money and take care of her family. At the same time, she looks to help those around her in the community. She first became involved with Marketplace Literacy Project when some University of Illinois students interviewed her as part of a project on health-related education.

Rahamat: Reshaping Her Destiny

The students asked Rahamat if she would consider buying health education materials at a certain price. She was silent for a moment and then gave a slight smile.

"I would buy it not for myself, but for others," she said. "I would buy it and teach others about it."

The students saw her as a potential customer. Rahamat saw a potential business venture.

"Everything I see," she says, "I see through the lens of an opportunity for business. An opportunity to buy and resell, to provide goods or services."

Ask her where she learned to look at the world in that way, and she quickly responds it came from necessity, when her husband died. As she now teaches other young women, she learned to fight. She learned to scrap and sacrifice, to plan and save.

She learned how to reshape what promised to be a hard destiny.

Her days are not filled with luxury, but neither are they filled with despair, hopelessness, and want. They are filled with hope, and confidence, and energy, and purpose.

~~~

Her children are, by and large, doing well. Her elder daughter, along with her two children, live at home with Rahamat; the daughter does not get along with her in-laws. This daughter has a steady job as a cashier. Her youngest son also lives with her at home.

Her younger daughter is a schoolteacher. Her oldest son, who completed 10th grade (all the others completed high school) works in the footwear trade, as does the youngest son. They both work for Rahamat's nephew, who owns his own business.

She has, in a sense, expanded her family; a tight bond between her and the 20 women in her self-help group exists.

"I moved from survival to subsistence to beyond," she says. "My goal now is to give back to my community around me."

The women in her self-help group sell saris. They are guided in their efforts by Rahamat, who collects Rs. 100 every month from each woman and deposits it in a joint bank account.

"We give loans, some small, some big, for children's education," she says, "and the bank helps us when needs arise. We also give money to our women during their time of delivery."

The women in the group find strength from each other and from Rahamat, their leader. They know what she has been through. They know she has not only walked to the mountain, but scaled it. They know that, along the way, she has overcome many challenges. They know she has come out on top, and they want to learn from her, follow her example, be like her.

"I can empathize with them," she says of the women in her group. "If my confidence and courage helps them get over their difficulties, then I should help them. I should not get tired of going to the bank often. We cannot expect any benefit or gain from the money that people have invested. What I can expect is that my words will give strength to those who are facing problems. I can motivate women not to lose courage. I can show them how to run a sari or pickle business."

One thing she has learned, both in her time in Ras al-Khaimah and in Saudi Arabia and in Qatar and in starting her own business back in India, is not to worry about things beyond her control. Instead, she focuses on what she *can* control - her attitude, her determination, her work ethic, her business sense.

"During seasonal time," she says, "I can earn ten thousand rupees per month [about $145 USD]. If I get the products for thirty thousand rupees, I can sell each sari for ten rupees profit [about 15 cents profit]. If it is not seasonal time, then I will not make as much profit."

The key word there is *profit*. Sometimes not a lot, but it's there. And it's enough, even in dry times.

Enough to buy a house and land. Enough to help her children and her mother out. Enough to get her business going and keep it going.

But for Rahamat, she is not content with enough. Her entrepreneur's eye is still roving, still on the lookout for additional opportunities.

"I am eager to do this on a larger scale," she says. "I want to go up. I hate to come down."

Up is the only direction Rahamat knows. Because going up is the only way to scale the mountains that you face.

And to reshape your destiny, you have to scale the mountain in front of you.

Growing Up Muslim in a Hindu Society

India is predominantly a Hindu country; it is about 81 percent Hindu, while the second most followed religion, Islam, is at about 13 percent. Rahamat is a devout Muslim; her beliefs and her faith are integral to all that she does. She begins and ends every day with prayers, and she relies on Islamic law to guide her in decision-making. For example, she will not criticize government leaders, because Islamic law forbids doing so.

Rahamat on Meeting the Challenges of Life

We asked Rahamat what made her such a good salesperson.

"I learned by experience, by trial and error," she said. "I had no choice. I learned by necessity. Otherwise I would not make the sale and we would have no money."

That's the same with other challenges in her life. They rose up in front of her and she had to find ways to overcome them. "My mother told me there are no shortcuts in life," she says. "She said I must be confident and strong."

She had to call on strength when she was forced to leave her children to go to work in another country: "It was very difficult for me to keep my children under somebody's care, but I didn't have any other way," she says. "I didn't have any male member to support my family. Till their marriage I am doing the role of both male and female."

As for working in a foreign country, she says, "I had no freedom there. It was really a challenge. Only with my confidence and courage I could get over those difficulties."

Today she faces the challenge of continuing to work past what most Westerners would consider retirement age, and doing so while battling diabetes. She gets a paltry 1000 rupees (around $15 USD) per month from the Indian government. But she accepts this reality with the equanimity—and the faith—that has served her throughout her life. "It is not up to the government to take care of me in this final chapter of my life. It is up to God."

Motivated to Succeed—and to Help Others Succeed

During our conversations with Rahamat, we discovered three primary motivations that have governed her actions in life:

- the desire to be responsible for her own health and wellbeing ("I don't want to sit idle," she told us. "I want to do something creatively so that my body will cooperate with me in the future");

- the desire to help others (she has mentored numerous young women who are facing hardships and has been running a self-help group for women for six years); and

- securing her children's, and now her grandchildren's, future.

21

Speaking with Rahamat outside and inside her
household in Chennai, India.

Rahamat's kitchen.

Chapter 2

Jaya: "I Would Like To Die A Peaceful Death"

"Surviving, day in and day out, is an exhausting existence. It is a constant drag on both body and spirit. And so you understand when she says, "I have seen a lot. I want my life to end when I am healthy and completely okay. I don't want to be a burden to others. I don't have any desire to live a long life. I would like to die a peaceful death."

Jaya's eyes are strong and clear; her smile, when she flashes it, is bright. She gives the appearance of one with great inner strength, and when you hear her story, you understand how that strength was given ample opportunity to develop.

Jaya is in her late 40s. She is in the best work situation of her life; she is a four-kilometer bus ride from an IT Park in Chennai, in Tamil Nadu, India, where she works as a housekeeper, mopping and dusting and cleaning. She regularly alternates from the 6 a.m. to 2 p.m. shift to the noon to 8 p.m. shift. She doesn't mind alternating back and forth; she is happy for the regular work.

"I make 7200 rupees a month [about $105 USD]," she says. "My rent is 3500 a month [about $50 USD]."

When asked if her income is enough, she shrugs and gives us a matter-of-fact look. "It is not sufficient," she says, "but what to do?"

That is a question she is tired of asking. She has probably asked herself that question thousands of times, until she tired of asking it, because there were no clear answers.

23

Jaya: "I Would Like To Die A Peaceful Death"

Now, her answer is this: she gets up, she goes to work, she comes home, she watches television. She is attracted to the shows that are sad, that show people in desperate situations.

That is the kind of life that she relates best to.

"I do not want to live a long life," she says.

~~~

Jaya lives alone in a tiny one-room apartment that has a few narrow shelves for clothes and a small TV. She sleeps on the floor on a thin mat. Her sole furniture is a small table with two mismatched chairs. She has two daughters, an older one who is in a tough marriage and who regularly asks her mother for monetary help, and a younger one in a better situation who looks after her mother and gives her "pocket money."

Her parents, who were a help to her when they were alive, are gone. A brother is dead. Her husband died. Worst of all, her youngest daughter died as well.

All deaths are very hard. But some deaths even more so.

Take, for instance, her husband's death. He did not die of an infection, or a disease, or an accident. His death was brought on by the darkness in his own heart. He did not work. He drank incessantly. He was both physically and verbally abusive to Jaya, who was only 14 when she married him and 15 when she bore her first of three girls. He was a drunkard and a tyrant, and Jaya often took the girls to her parents' house to live. But her mother kept telling her to return to her husband. It was the right thing to do.

So Jaya would reluctantly return. Nothing would change. He would drink. He would terrorize her. He would beat and berate her. He would demand food. What money he could scrape up was spent on alcohol. Fatherhood, for him, ended with the act of conceiving.

One time Jaya returned home and another woman was living with her husband.

"Who is this woman?" she demanded. The woman shrank back from Jaya, retreating to a corner of the room. She had been tending a small fire to cook with while he sat in a chair drinking from a bottle of *sunda kanji*, a sort of "rice beer" made from fermenting rice that is buried in earthen pots and that is popular among the poor in Tamil Nadu.

"It is none of your business who it is. You are never here," he responded. He did not even have the decency to look at Jaya. She saw it in his eyes. He is the king of his house. He can do as he pleases. Anger flared in her own eyes.

"You tell her to leave now. She cannot be in my house."

"This is my house too. It is my house first. Then it is your house. But you were not even here. I will invite anyone into my house that I want."

"You tell her to leave right now or I will kick you both out. Then you will see what it is like to live on the street, like a dog."

Enraged, he rose quickly and grabbed her by both her wrists. He then struck her across her face and spat on her and shoved her toward the fire. She put out her hand to break her fall and shrieked as her palm was burned. She cried out in agony and, with him still yelling at her, she stumbled out of the house and made her way, her vision blurred with tears and her hand in extreme pain, to get treatment.

She took her girls back to her parents' house after getting her hand treated. Her mother was shocked at the wrapping on her hand and at her story. Her father wanted to go throw her husband out of the house, but Jaya stopped him. "I want nothing to do with him ever again," she said. "Do not waste your time on him, as I have."

Within a few weeks, word drifted back to her. The family of the young woman her husband had taken into their home had come and demanded that he return the woman to them. He refused. Shouting and threats ensued. Two of the woman's brothers scuffled with Jaya's husband, but nothing more happened.

But three days later they returned to Jaya's home. Again they demanded the return of the woman. Again Jaya's husband refused. Again threats were issued and ignored. And again a scuffle broke out.

But this time the scuffle was more serious. This time the men beat Jaya's husband. They beat him hard, and he stood no chance against them. Their rage did not abate. As her husband fell to the floor in his home, they continued beating him. One of the brothers kicked him, hard, in the head. They heard him groan. They issued more kicks to the midsection, the back, the head.

Jaya's husband stopped groaning. He lay dead on his own floor, and the two brothers grabbed their sister by the arm and jerked her out of the house.

~~~

Jaya went to the mortuary where her husband's body lay. She had to struggle, she says, to retrieve his body and perform the rituals that are commonly performed by Hindus. She bathed his body and put sacred ash on the body as a priest chanted holy mantras. Before the body was cremated, she put rice in the mouth (nourishment for the departed soul), flowers on the body, and a coin in each hand. The body was then taken to the crematorium.

And so Jaya entered into an uncertain new phase in her life. She was 23, barely beyond childhood herself, now widowed and responsible for the welfare of her three young daughters. Yes, she was freed from a bad marriage, but she had her girls to provide for, and she had no money in savings and no steady work.

She knew one thing: that she was finished with the neighborhood and the house in which so much pain had been inflicted on her. She wanted to, needed to, move beyond that pain. And so she and her girls went to live with her parents.

~~~

But she was not, as she soon discovered, finished with pain itself. Tragedy seemed to stalk her. Her older brother, after arguing with his wife and perhaps feeling trapped and without hope for either the present or the future, killed himself. Her parents, who were good to her daughters, died one by one. After they died, Jaya and her girls lived for a while with another brother, but her sister-in-law's harsh words toward her drove her out.

Jaya rented the house next to her parents' old house, and struggled to make ends meet, earning Rs. 200 ($3.00 USD) doing domestic work in the houses of middle- and upper-middle class families, cooking, cleaning, doing laundry. "I barely had enough money to buy rice," she says, adding that some of her employers gave her food to take home. "But my daughters did not eat much, so we were okay." Through her work, she managed to save a bit of money in a chit fund and purchased some simple jewels for her oldest daughter in preparation for her future marriage (bridal jewelry is a revered custom in India, even among the poorest of the poor).

Her first two daughters stopped school in 6th and 7th grades, going to work to help keep a roof over their heads and food on their table. They were following in Jaya's own footsteps; she finished 6th grade before finding work to help her parents. Among the poor in India, this is a common road to take.

The youngest daughter stayed in school until 9th grade and then she too went to work, as a tailor in an export company. She worked for two years for the company, but her supervisor was a harsh and unforgiving man.

27

Jaya: "I Would Like To Die A Peaceful Death"

Jaya's youngest had a sensitive heart. She worked hard. She wanted to keep her job. She knew how important the money was to her family. While her father had never given her encouragement, her mother had, and her teachers had. She was a good student and that was in part why she stayed in school until 9th grade. She would have stayed longer, but her family needed the income. And so she worked, willingly.

But she was not used to criticism, especially harsh criticism. She was not used to people yelling at her for being slow in her work or making minor mistakes. She was not used to being constantly watched, constantly upbraided. The eyes of her supervisor bore into her soul and tormented her. He was constantly critical of her. One day he harangued her for wasting a bit of cloth. The cloth cost money. Everything that was wasted meant money out of their own pockets. She was a worthless girl who paid no attention to her work. She must improve her work or she would be fired. No one would want to hire her. He would tell other employees that she was worthless.

The words rained down on her like sulfur. Emotionally it burned her deeply and irreparably. She ran home that afternoon and, with no one home, she found a rope and, at the tender age of 17, she hung herself.

~~~

Jaya wept and wept over her daughter. This was her precious child, her youngest. Jaya had had such hopes for her, such pride in her. Now she laid her daughter out to prepare her for her final journey, as she had done her husband many years earlier. But the feeling was vastly different. With her husband, the ritual she performed was a duty, an obligation. There was no love lost between them. There was only relief, and sadness — not at losing the man who made her life miserable, but at the missed opportunity of a happy marriage, where each person

28

supported and encouraged and loved the other. Her movements in preparing her husband were mechanical, programmed.

But with her youngest daughter, as Jaya tenderly washed the body, still smooth and supple and hardy, she felt such heartache that she wanted to die. Jaya's own tears mixed with the water that cleansed the body. With trembling hands, she placed the body in a robe, and tied the robe around the waist, and laid flowers on the young chest and stomach, and placed the rice in the mouth and the coins in the hands. The priest chanted his mantras, but Jaya did not hear them. She heard the sound of her now dead daughter's laughter, the laughter of a toddler, of a young girl. She heard the questions of a young girl asking her mother questions in the marketplace—what vegetables those were, what did they taste like, could they get a piece of candy on their way home. Just one piece. Please?

As the body was about to be carried to the crematorium, Jaya fell first to her knees, then to all fours. Sobs racked her body, which shook silently for a while, like a volcano ready to burst, and then the sobs came out in volume. The sounds of grief filled the tiny house and spilled out into the road and were heard by all who passed by. And people who had been in friendly conversation stopped talking, and looked solemnly at each other, and passed Jaya's house, silently, out of respect.

It is no different in India than anywhere else in the world. It is no different for rich people or poor people, for the highly literate or the low-literate. The same holds true across the world. No mother should have to bury her young daughter, and any mother who does so does not fully recover. She goes on, but she does not recover.

~~~

Jaya had not only the loss of her daughter to deal with, but the loss of her daughter's income as well. The financial shift necessitated a search for a better-paying job; her current income as a domestic would not stretch to cover both rent and food expenses. Her search uncovered the position she has been in for the past 10 years now, working as a housekeeper. The job was gained through a contract agency and includes a provident fund (she contributes 10 percent of her monthly wages and the company matches that contribution in a savings fund) and health insurance. Her contract is for five years and can be extended to remain with the same company, or she might be placed with a new company at the end of the contract. Either way, it is a better situation than her former domestic work.

Jaya's oldest daughter is in a marriage that was arranged by Jaya's mother. It is not a happy marriage, much like Jaya's own marriage. The husband is a drunkard and does little work to support his wife and their two children. This daughter is repeating the mistake that Jaya unwittingly made, and it is hard for Jaya to see her daughter in such a marriage.

"He takes all her money for drinking," she says, remembering that scenario well from her own life. "He is a burden to her. And whenever she comes to visit, it is only for money. She comes asking for 10,000 rupees. I cannot give her that amount. She comes all the time asking, pleading. She wants me to buy saris for her, other things. She only wants things from me." (Jaya has offered to have her daughter and her children move in with her, but they have refused. Jaya would love to be more involved in the lives of this daughter's children. She would like to help them stay away from bad influences, but, as with her daughter, the grandchildren do not listen to her. Thus, she does not see them at festivals and does not give them money for the festivals.)

Ten thousand rupees is about $145 USD. She has, in savings, about 25,000 rupees ($364 USD), painstakingly put away over the past few decades. It is the money she has to live on past retirement. She did not remarry and has no one to take care of her. Traditionally, widows in India do not remarry, though that tradition is weakening some, and her father encouraged her to remarry because she and her children were so young when her husband was killed, but Jaya was adamant. "I told him I will not remarry. I did not want a new husband who would torture my children. So I didn't think about remarrying."

Jaya's second daughter is also married, living in Chennai with her husband and two sons. Her husband works in a shoe leather company and the daughter is a housewife. This daughter is helpful to Jaya, and she has taken her mother on pilgrimage for five days as part of a tour group, for which the daughter paid.

"She gives me some pocket money," Jaya says. "She takes care of me." Jaya says that she recently had to go to the hospital to be treated for dysentery. "A drip was given, and my daughter took care of me and also gave me money," she says. "She supports me."

Jaya, too, helps support this daughter, giving her money during festivals and in times of stress.

~~~

So much of what Jaya had hoped for has not transpired. She wanted a better life for herself. She wanted a good, strong marriage, a husband who would love and support her and help her raise her children. She wanted better, longer educations for her daughters. She wanted her daughters to marry good husbands. (The second one has.)

Jaya is, above all, a survivor. She has survived a cruel and broken husband; a man who tried to break her, too. She has survived the suicides of her youngest daughter and her older brother. She has survived being a young widow with no money and three children to raise. She has survived the sometime savage twists and turns that each day brings to those who live in subsistence. She has survived the long nights of wondering and praying about the welfare of her children. She has survived the long days of working diligently and hard and being paid

31

very little for it. She has survived the many disappointments that have come her way.

But surviving, day in and day out, is an exhausting existence. It is a constant drag on both body and spirit. And so you understand when she says, "I have seen a lot. I want my life to end when I am healthy and completely okay. I don't want to be a burden to others. I don't have any desire to live a long life. I would like to die a peaceful death."

~~~

Despite the sentiment that Jaya expressed about a peaceful death, she is far from glum. In fact, we have witnessed a fresh hope and energy in her in recent visits (we have interviewed Jaya several times over the years).

On one recent visit, we learned that many things had changed in her life—some for the better, and some that brought on fresh challenges and concerns.

On the plus side, she moved from her tiny one-room apartment to a larger one, because her old landlord increased the rent from Rs. 1000 to Rs. 3500. Her new apartment is brighter; her daughter helped her install a fan and lights. She was beaming as we entered her new apartment and she humbly and gratefully received our compliments on her new living arrangements. Jaya is a most gracious host with a wonderful gift of hospitality that makes her apartment seem even brighter. In anticipation of our visit, she had used rice powder to make a welcome sign for us outside of her apartment. She also eagerly showed us off to her neighbors, who insisted on being photographed with us.

Inside her apartment, the first thing she showed us was a large photo of her daughter who had committed suicide. It is part of Jaya's shrine in her home.

Voices From Subsistence Marketplaces

The next thing that Jaya showed us was her work ID — you could see how greatly she treasured this card, which identified her as an employee in a respectable information technology park. She is respected in her work, which she approaches with diligence and care. To be respected in her work means the world to her.

"Last year I had to miss a month and a half of work due to an injury," she told us, "but the company still gave me partial pay." Such treatment was far from her experience when, as a married teenager, she crushed rocks for meager pay. Still beaming, she retrieved a pay stub and showed it to us. To receive an actual pay stub, to be respected and to be paid even when she was off for an injury — such things were beyond her imagination earlier in her life.

She also proudly told us that she had voted in a recent national election. "Our company encourages us to vote," she said. "They give us time off from work to do so."

On the down side, she was ill during the previous year, and her daughter had a kidney tumor. Mentioning this, she said, "My goals are good health and a year in which I do not have to borrow from others." During her illness, she made three trips to temples; her daughter helped her with the Rs. 2000 that she spent for these visits. In return, Jaya gave her daughter a washing machine, hoping it would lighten her work and improve her daughter's health.

Jaya's life is filled with the ups and downs of those who live in subsistence. She has had much sorrow and hardship in her life. It was good to see her in a nicer apartment, with a job she was respected in and well treated. She takes each day as it comes, facing it with equanimity and a hope that her current state continues until a peaceful death.

Jaya with a picture she keeps to remember her youngest daughter.

Inside Jaya's home.

Madhu and John (Authors) with Jaya and her neighbor.

Chapter 3

Shanthi: Finding Strength Outside The Home

"It would be a pleasure to go out. Otherwise I would be inside the house within four walls. Outside, I could learn a lot."

Shanthi's eyes sparkle like peaceful jewels. She has a calm about her, a serenity, and at first glance, this woman from a tiny village in southeast India would not seem to have the chutzpah to run her own business, or to travel to Spencer Plaza, a landmark in Chennai, to barter with male merchants. Chennai, after all, is the fourth-largest metropolitan area in India, and the country is very much a patriarchal society.

Underneath that calm exterior, however, is the bubbling excitement of a child: Spencer Plaza! To Shanthi, Spencer Plaza is an almost mythical place, a place she never would have dreamed of traveling to—and bartering in—earlier in her life. To her it is an exotic and thrilling place to be, teeming with life and sparkling with possibilities; she feels not unlike a Western child making her first visit to Disneyland. To the Westerner's eye, Spencer Plaza is an old-fashioned, unexciting shopping center; to Shanthi, it represents a new and exciting way of life.

So here is this frail, bespectacled woman, with her serene Mona Lisa smile, traveling to this bustling plaza to talk to merchants and show them her wares: beautifully handcrafted and precisely painted papier mâché dolls of all sizes. The dolls set on a stand, and, being made of four parts, bob and move as you touch them.

A heavyset merchant with bristly chin hair and black-framed glasses whose long temples are perched two inches above his ears, so that the lenses are slanted toward his nose, holds a six-inch doll in his hands, slowly turning it around. Shanthi watches the man's eyes, trying to read his thoughts, but the man's eyes are hooded. Finally he looks up very noncommittally.

"Okay," he says. "I will take one dozen for Rs. 500 each [about $7.30 USD]."

The calmness does not leave her eyes, but something in them sharpens. She gives him a little smile.

"No sir, those we cannot sell for less than Rs. 1100 [about $16 USD]. Do you see the quality?"

He gives the doll another guarded look and then shrugs his shoulders.

"Okay, today is your lucky day," he says. "I will pay Rs. 600 each."

Shanthi's eyes gleam brightly as she watches the merchant for a moment before, still with that small smile on her face, she takes the doll from him and begins to place it in its cardboard box.

"I will move on, sir," she says, and she begins to walk away.

"Wait!" the merchant calls out.

She returns. They talk some more. They end on a price of Rs. 900 (about $13 USD). That is the price she had in mind, and she was willing to go from merchant to merchant until she got it. (Shanthi tells us that the seller will likely add 50 percent to what he paid for the dolls when he sells it to his customers. Bargaining is a way of life in India, and if you do not possess good bargaining skills, you will be paying higher prices and selling for lower prices than you need to. Developing bargaining skills is an important facet of Indian life, particularly at the subsistence level.)

All of this, understand, is amazing for a rural Indian woman with a 5th grade education. And nearly as surprising is the attitude of her husband, who, as Shanthi says, "accepts" her working outside the home—

not exactly a ringing endorsement, but also far from the norm in traditional India and a sign of the changing times as well.

~~~

Shanthi married her maternal uncle long ago – she is in her mid-fifties now – and they lived for a time in Mayiladudurai in Chennai. (Marrying maternal uncles is a common cultural practice in certain communities in this part of India.) But when her mother-in-law died, Shanthi and her husband found it hard to manage with their three boys, and her parents asked her to come to the small village about 80 kilometers south of Chennai where they have lived since 1985. Her husband continues to work for the export company, ironing clothes, a job he has worked at for the past 26 years.

"My parents gave us a plot, and we constructed a house in that plot and we are still living there," she says.

Her parents giving them that plot of land was one big turning point in Shanthi's life. Perhaps an even bigger one occurred in 1990, when her oldest son was in eighth grade. Without more funds, he would not be able to enter ninth grade.

So Shanthi joined with nine other women in her village and, under the guidance and help of Mr. Umapathy, a village leader, they created a self-help group and formed a cooperative to make and sell papier mâché dolls. She put in 10,000 rupees (about $145 USD) as an initial investment, which she has long since recovered.

"When I began working," Shanthi says, "I was making seven rupees a day [about 10 cents]. Now I am making 5,000 rupees a month [about $73 USD]." It was enough to keep her son in school, and it is enough now to help with her grandchildren's education.

Shortly before helping to form the co-op, Shanthi learned to paint through a 6-month course offered by the government for the village women. The women put their newfound skills to use. Mr. Umapathy petitioned the government for a bit of land for a building, and a loan to build, and the small house that in reality is their doll factory was built in 2000 and paid off in 2007, thanks to a cash reserve that the coop was able to save.

In the beginning they were producing five or six dolls a day. Now the women carefully and expertly craft and paint 200 to 250 dolls a week. Shanthi notes that there are four stages in doll-making, from blending the mixture to molding the various body parts to assembling the parts to painting them; she began in the molding section, but has an allergy to the wallpaper powder used in the papier mâché, and so moved to painting about a dozen years ago. "I choose the colors, I choose the styles," she says. "But if a customer has an idea, I can paint it as they want it."

As she worked in the doll business, life continued with its ups and downs around her. All three sons stopped at 10th grade, though she encouraged them to continue and had the money through her work to support their studies. Unable to talk them into furthering their education, she tried to get them to go to work for a company in a nearby industrial complex. But they are all working as drivers for companies near their village. So she helped them buy vehicles, taking a loan from her brother and a few others to aid the purchases. Her oldest son got married, and he and his wife and two daughters live with her and her husband.

That set of disappointments pales with the heartbreak she endured a few years ago, when her youngest son drowned while swimming in a pond with his friends. It is only as she recounts this that the light from her eyes dims, as if a cloud is passing over. The ever-present serene smile fades as well. We are interviewing her in her doll shop, in her painting room; several doll frames are on a table in varying degrees of completion.

Shanthi idly fingers a doll, looking down, and then she looks back up, the shine returning to her eyes. "My first granddaughter is seven years old," she says. "She is studying in second standard. My second granddaughter is two years old." She pauses, and then a sweet smile makes the dark cloud that had settled over her disperse. "If I have any problems or any stress," she says, "it just vanishes when I see my granddaughters' faces."

Becoming a businesswoman has done more for Shanthi than allow her to help her children and grandchildren. It has opened up an avenue for her to help other women who are trying to make a way for themselves or help their families. Taking strength from her self-help group and her work, Shanthi has begun to share the lessons she has learned with other women in the village and in her group. And she has started her own small home business by supplying the co-op with materials for the dolls. To start the business, she borrowed 10,000 rupees (about $145 USD) from her mother; she has paid off that loan.

Shanthi, you see, does not like to be in debt to anyone. She likes to be independent.

~~~

As with most any new business proposition, the coop faced challenges early on. The women had to acquire quality control skills to ensure that their dolls were of uniformly high quality. They had production challenges as well, learning to work together as a team in a coordinated fashion where the process was not bogged down in any one area. But to survive, they knew they needed to acquire these skills, and now they are an amazingly smooth unit, working seamlessly together, producing high quality merchandise.

They make small talk as they work, and you sense a comfortable, familial feel in the room as they work. They have worked together for many years now, and are as much sisters as they are friends. At their various posts, they waste no motion as they efficiently and methodically create the doughy substance, roll it out as if they were rolling out bread dough, and shape and mold it into the four doll parts (head, torso, long skirt, and base, which includes the legs and feet). Each part fits on top of the part below it. The finished doll then goes to Shanti to paint.

"I used to work with the powder," she says, "but I had to stop because my lungs were affected. So they put me to painting." In the painting room a few dozen dolls sit, each one a little different from the others. They are each a unique creation, and it is through these creations, the collective efforts of the ten women and Mr. Umapathy, that the women's lives are bettered. Through their creativity and resourcefulness, food is on the table. Children are sent to school. Cars are purchased. New businesses are begun. New dreams emerge.

~~~

One of those dreams, for Shanthi, is to do a bit of traveling. Other than a few trips to Chennai and some trips with her enterprise, she has stayed in her small village, worked in the co-op, raised her family, and is now helping to raise her granddaughters.

"Going to distant places would be an experience," she says. "It would be a pleasure to go out. I could learn a lot."

She does, however, derive much pleasure from the shorter trips she makes with her enterprise. On these trips, they train groups of 10 women each in how to make dolls. They help them understand not just the practicalities of making dolls, but of running a business - securing loans, buying the materials, pricing the dolls, getting them in the marketplace, and so on.

"The women we train are very enthusiastic," Shanthi says, smiling. "They are so excited to start their own business. They are very friendly and give us gifts for teaching them." Perhaps the women they train are enthusiastic in part because their teachers are eager to help them learn to start their own business. Shanthi takes special pleasure in helping other women acquire the know-how to start their own business, and she shares her expertise with all that she can, including her brother's wife. Shanthi has learned how to be independent and make her own income, and she knows how important this is to other women around her. She is as good a teacher, mentor, and coach as she is a doll maker.

Shanthi has spent nearly a quarter of a century making dolls. In taking the risk to step outside her home and invest in becoming part of a business, she has gained much and helped her family. Her husband supported her in her decision to work, and this is not always the case in India.

Over the years, she has learned the importance of taking a calculated risk. Had she not done that, her life, and the lives of her family, would be very different. She has also learned that she is capable, that she is skilled, that her work has value to it.

Perhaps most of all, she has learned that *she* has value. She has gained self-respect and an equanimity that helps her balance the good and the bad in life, the pleasant and the difficult. She has weathered a lot in her life, and in her 25 years of working, and, of lasting importance, she is teaching others in self-help groups how to step up, step out, and find their strength outside of their home, creating businesses that can help sustain them.

"A lot of people we have trained have gone on to start their own businesses," she says as she puts the finishing touches on a doll's skirt. She places her fine brush on the wood table, which has bits of many different colors on it, and smiles that enigmatic smile of hers.

"I am very proud and happy for them," she says. "As for me, I could not have done all this if I had been sitting at home and doing nothing."

Changes in Village Life

We have visited Shanthi over the years and we have noted some changes in her village. On a recent trip, we asked her about those changes.

"Oh yes, things have changed," she said. "Many things. There are more permanent dwellings now and fewer huts. That is good. We also have more shops with groceries, so it is easier to get our food. That too is good.

"But this growth has caused more trash, more clogged drains, and brought more mosquitoes. These are new problems our village faces. We are working to solve these problems."

Indeed, travelling to this semi-urban village year after year for about a decade, we have noticed steady changes over time, in terms of the improved house constructions and fewer huts. The progress seems to parallel with some lag, the general growth in an emerging economy.

She mentioned another significant change: Women are a large part of the group that is working to solve the village's problems. "Ten years ago, no women would be allowed to be involved in village issues," she said. "Now we are working to help solve the problems. And why shouldn't we? It is our village, they are our homes, too."

Shanthi posing for a picture
after an interview.

Shanthi standing outside the
community art center.

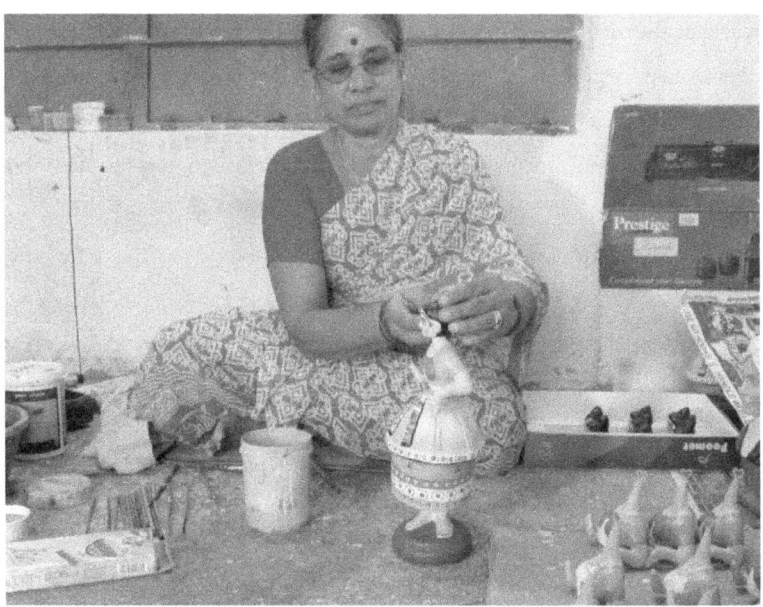

Shanthi constructs her dolls in her workspace.

Chapter 4

Lalitha: Business Equals Survival

"I can't afford to lose customers, sir. I can't afford to buy inferior products... I have a loyal customer base. There are many who know of my family situation. They come and buy from me."

Lalitha rises at 4 a.m. out of habit; she and her husband have internal alarm clocks in their bodies that for years awakened them to go work in the rice paddies around their village. She cleanses herself and dresses in a fresh salmon-colored sari and kneels to worship in front of the small shrine in a corner of her small house. The shrine has many pictures of gods, and icons, incense, and sacred candles. It is quiet; her husband and two sons are still sleeping.

After her prayers she touches her forehead to the floor and slowly rises to face her day.

Her days are long, and always start with worship, followed by caring for her twin sons. They are in their twenties, unable to walk, but able to use their arms and hands. She helps them get cleansed and dressed, and her husband rises, and she makes a breakfast for them consisting of rice or on some days idli, a kind of cake made from black lentils and rice.

This is how her days started last summer when we visited her. It is how they went long before we visited her. And it is how they will go long after this visit, probably until the end of her days.

44

Her primary goal in life is to make enough money to buy rice for her family.

But she does not just depend on government stipends to buy the rice.

She runs her own shop, which she goes to each morning after breakfast and tends throughout the day except when she has to return home to feed her twins and to make sure that the mat that they sit on all day is well positioned.

Her shop is about 100 meters from her home, on a dusty roadside. She received two loans, one from the government for 5000 rupees (about $72 USD by today's markets), the other from her women's self-help group, which she had to repay in ten months. With the loans, she built a mobile stall with a thatched roof for her shop, which sells packets of soaps and shampoos, candies and chocolates, toothpaste, spices, chips, bottled drinks, and small amounts of petrol for the many motorbikes that travel the dirt roads. Because there is no door to the shop, she must carry her products home at the end of each day, and bring them back to the shop each morning.

100 Days of Work, Guaranteed

India's National Rural Employment Guarantee Act of 2005 offers 100 days of wage employment per year to every household whose adult members volunteer to do unskilled manual labor. Lalitha takes advantage of this act, which has since been renamed the Mahatma Gandhi National Rural Employment Guarantee Act. The act is aimed directly at people and families living in subsistence, and while the act is not without its administrative and implementation problems, it has been of benefit to many living in subsistence in India.

~~~

Lalitha: Business Equals Survival

I meet her at her shop one warm summer morning.

"Good morning, Lalitha, how are you?" I ask, smiling.

She returns the smile and says "Good sir, very good, thank you."

She goes about setting up her shop and we make small talk. As she finishes placing her products on the shelves of her shop wall, I say, "How much profit do you make in a day at your shop?"

"Sir, I hope to make forty rupees profit each day," she says. This is about 60 cents.

She sees a bit of concern in my eyes and puts it in context for me.

"Before, I made only twenty rupees profit. But when I got the stall, it went up."

Her expansion in profits came about fortuitously. The landowner where she previously sold her goods – under a tree across the road from her house – told her she could not sell there anymore.

"So what did you do?" I ask.

"I went to see Vijayan. I told him my problem. He helped me."

"Who is Vijayan?"

"He is a village leader, sir. He gave me permission to set up my shop here, and helped me get a government loan for it."

(Village leaders are often the first and last line of support in resolving conflicts and connecting to the outside world. Vijayan is a unique leader who genuinely cares about his community and helps the people nearby). Her shop is now about 100 meters from her house. So what was initially bad news – being kicked off the land where she previously sold her goods – became good news and sparked an upgrade in her shop and an increase in sales.

Lalitha's husband does not have steady work. He works in the fields on occasions when extra helpers are needed – which is not often. Lalitha is, to paraphrase an American term, the rice-winner in her family. Her twins will never walk or work. Her family is totally dependent on her profit of 20 to 40 rupees a day.

And those rupees do not come easily, because she has competitors up and down the road. Many women are doing the same thing Lalitha is doing – selling small products to earn enough money to put rice on the table.

"I can't afford to lose customers, sir," she says, and I see the fear in her eyes at such a prospect. "I can't afford to buy inferior products."

As we talk, a customer comes and buys some toothpaste, a packet of soap, and some candies. Lalitha converses with the older gentleman, thanking him for his business. He smiles and nods at her, and then gives her a little wave as he walks off.

"You have done business with him before," I say.

"Oh yes, sir. I have a loyal customer base," she says. "There are many who know of my family situation. They come and buy from me."

~~~

Tamil is the language that Lalitha speaks. The colloquial word in Tamil for *business* is *pozhaipu*, which can be translated as *survival*.

That is exactly what business is for Lalitha.

She learned many business principles through the Marketplace Literacy Communities, a nonprofit organization which educates low-literate, low-income people about the practices of businesses, governments, not-for-profit organizations, and educators. Through MLC, Lalitha learned to buy, to sell, to survive by being an entrepreneur. This experience has helped her survive—in terms of self-confidence, skills, and awareness of rights.

"I never imagined I could run a shop on my own," she says as two young girls, shy but giggling, purchase a few candies from her. As the girls skip down the road, happy in their purchase, she says, "I watched others who ran small shops, and one day I thought that would be a good thing for my family. I thought it was something maybe I could do."

Lalitha: Business Equals Survival

While she was running her roadside shop before she attended an MLC training that took place in Uthiremerur, what she learned in the training gave her greater confidence and know-how in running her business.

~~~

She now has the means to survive for today, but she still prefers not to think of the future. The burden of keeping food on the table is daunting. Another burden on her heart is her sons, who are hampered by severe disabilities. They will never get married, unlike her other three children, who are married and living in nearby villages. That saddens her. It also worries her to think of what will happen to them when she is gone, because she is the one they depend on.

To illustrate this, you need only see the two broken-down wheelchairs sitting outside of their home. They were given to the family by a nonprofit that visited the village. But of course the infrastructure of the village and of the home made wheelchairs highly impractical, and they broke down within a few weeks. By this time the nonprofit was long gone and the chairs are a dust-gathering reminder that the help that is most useful is that which is both practical and permanent.

But Lalitha does not allow herself to worry about her sons when she is gone. Those are tomorrow's problems. Today brings enough troubles of its own. Any talk of the future elicits a quick shake of the head from her.

"I don't want to think about it," she says, and she turns to tend to something, even if there is nothing to tend to.

This puts into context a fear that she one time expressed to me: the fear of debt. Her fear was that if she were to receive a loan of 50 rupees – about 73 cents – she would never be able to pay it back.

The fear that she felt at such a prospect was palpable.

~~~

Some days Lalitha must take off work to take her sons to Uthiremerur, a village about a 30-minute bus ride away from her own tiny village. Uthiremerur is also the place where she purchases her soaps and candies and other goods that she sells in her shop.

Besides those brief visits for her sons' medical needs and to restock her store, her shop is open – 7 days a week, 365 days a year. Come rain, come shine, Lalitha is always in her shop.

Because her shop, her business, is survival.

She has a TV in her house – almost all Indian homes seem to have TVs – but she never watches it. (While her TV was given to her by the state government—an election-time promise actually made good on— you can also buy a new, conventional television for $60 USD or less. Nearly 150 million of the 192 million households in India have cable TV. For about 1000 rupees you can get 250 or more channels. A basic package costs about 250 rupees, or about $4 USD.) She doesn't want to see the news and hear of other people's problems. She has enough of her own. She has never been to Chennai, the capital of Tamil Nadu, less than two hours away by car. For her it might as well be a million miles away.

She has no business in Chennai. Her business is 100 meters from her home in her village.

"Do you want to travel?" I asked her one day.

"No sir, why would I want to travel?"

I shrugged and smiled. "To see other things. To enjoy the world, to take a brief break from your work."

She looked at me as if I were crazy. "No sir, I do not need to see other things. I need to be here, tending my shop."

When Lalitha began her business, she had neither mentors nor experience to lean on. She just had hope, and a desire to survive.

49

She took that hope and desire and turned it into something practical.

To say she runs her business on a shoestring budget would not be overstating the case. She operates from day to day, making 20 rupees (about 29 cents) one day, 35 the next. Maybe 55 one day, but 0 the next, as she takes her sons for medical treatment.

She keeps her focus squarely on the day in front of her. She looks neither left nor right, neither backward nor forward.

And at the end of the day, she returns home, makes dinner, says her prayers in front of the shrine, and lets sleep give her a break from her day's work.

That is all the break she needs, or wants.

Living on the Edge

Living in subsistence means you are always living on the edge; one thing can drastically tip the scales against you.

For example, Lalitha told us about a time when one of her handicapped sons took ill. They had to spend 700 rupees (about $10 USD) to hire a car to take him to the hospital. Her eldest son, who works as an electrician, paid for the car and the hospital expenses. A blood test at the cost of 250 rupees (about $4 USD) determined that the son had a rat-based fever. He was hospitalized for one week. Lalitha stayed in the hospital with her son while her husband watched the shop. Had Lalitha not had the assistance she received from her eldest son, she and her family could have easily been tipped from survival to starvation.

The Cost of a Smile of Gratitude: Priceless

You've seen the MasterCard commercials: You add up the money it took to go on some meaningful venture. You account for travel costs, lodging, tickets, meals, whatever. And at the end you measure the cost of what you *gained* from that experience. And the answer is always, "Priceless."

Well, I had a priceless experience with Lalitha. I had visited her before and when I returned, I brought with me a photograph of her that I had taken the year before. It cost me 17 cents to reproduce.

When I handed it to her she had tears of gratitude in her eyes and a big smile on her face. She thanked me and I was deeply moved by her gratitude. She later told Madhu, the architect and mastermind behind Marketplace Literacy Communities and behind all the travel to and work in subsistence communities, that she had met many visitors as a result of her involvement with Marketplace Literacy Communities, but none understood her or her life's circumstances as well as I did.

That brought tears to my eyes. And for any financial or other sacrifices I had made in traveling many times to India for this work, the payback I got from Lalitha made it more than worthwhile.

It made it priceless.

--*John Hedeman*

Lalitha outside her home.

Lalitha's small shop and her
husband (in the white shirt)

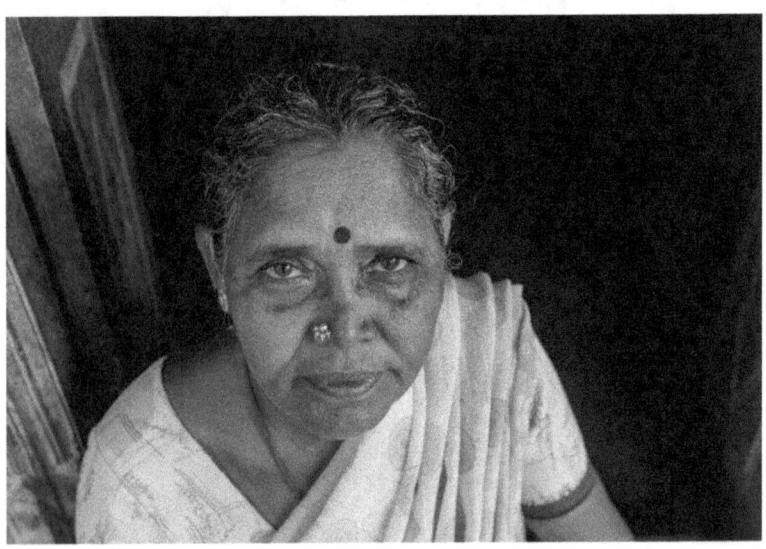

Bottom photo: Alpana Aras-King | www.alpanaaras.com

Alpana Aras | www.alpanaaras.com

Alpana Aras | www.alpanaaras.com

Chapter 5

Sigamani: "Aside From Children, What Else Is There?"

"Yes sir," he says. "And if my children are fine, then it is fine with me. I don't want anything else."

"Nothing else?"

"Aside from children, what else is there?"

As we drive to a village a few hours south of Chennai, we talk about what Sigamani might have experienced since we have seen him last. We are excited to see him again, as it has been a few years since our last visit.

Sigamani and his family live in a yellow brick house in a village in the south of Tamil Nadu. It is a house he is proud of, and for good reason.

Until 2003, he and his family – his wife and son and two daughters (one of whom is now married and living in a nearby village) – lived in a thatched hut. Such huts are common in rural India. They offer shelter from a storm and little else.

Now they live in a brick house, built thanks to a Rs. 75,000 (about $110 USD) government grant and to additional money borrowed from a moneylender from a particular caste who lives in Sigamani's village. He borrowed Rs. 10,000, about $145 USD, and pays monthly interest of Rs. 2-3 per Rs. 100 borrowed.

His son has also put his own money into upgrading the house. Sigamani's son has painstakingly worked on the house over the years, refurbishing and expanding it. It is luxurious compared to the hut they used to live in, and it has tiles of Hindu deities in front, to ward off evil.

We know from our previous visit that Sigamani takes his religion seriously, though he does not like to talk about it. Indeed, the scent of devotion and faith hangs heavy in the air in and around his home.

We leave our footwear outside the house. This is an Indian tradition and has both sanitary and religious significance.

Inside, we greet his wife. She has been ill but neither of them like to discuss her health. So we respect that, and Sigamani gives us a brief tour of his small house.

As we tour the house, we note that there is no bathroom. We are informed that essentially no one in the village has an indoor toilet. Later, outside, Sigamani points to some bushes along the side of the road. The women, he says, go to the toilet on the left, the men on the right.

~~~

Inside his house, the first room Sigamani takes us to is a "Saami room," one dedicated to the gods and to worship. We see many pictures and statues of gods, and we also see that this is the room where he stores his two drums, indicating the importance the drums play in his life. Sigamani has been a barber his whole adult life, but he is most alive when he is playing the drums.

His eyes light up when we ask him to play the drums. He picks them up, wraps the thick drum band around his back, and begins to play. The sound that comes from the drums, which are covered in cowhide, is rich and deep. He tells us that he plays for temple festivals, marriage ceremonies, and death ceremonies. He adds that he plays with other musicians, some of whom play trumpet-like instruments, at these ceremonies.

"They come from different villages," he says. "They call me on my mobile phone when there is a job in their village, and I do the same when there is an assignment in my village."

If you think it odd that a man who by all accounts is very poor and who has lived most of his life in a thatched hut has a mobile phone, know that in India mobile phones are cheaply purchased and ubiquitous.

How ubiquitous? In India, there are more than 874 million mobile phone users (out of a population of about 1.2 billion people). Nearly 73 percent of the population has a mobile phone. By contrast, only about 33 percent of the population has access to toilets.

The Use of Mobile Phones in Rural India

The influx of mobile phones in rural India since 2000 is phenomenal. In 2000, less than 1 percent of rural Indians owned mobile phones. By 2010, that had grown to 22 percent. By 2015, it was close to 75 percent. It is undoubtedly even higher today.

Some people might find it surprising that a significant and growing percent of impoverished rural Indians own mobile phones. Here are some of the factors that have contributed to the rise in mobile phone usage:

- Rural Indians have a number of inexpensive phones to choose from.
- The phones are often used as literal lifelines that connect ill people with the emergency services that they need to address medical problems that otherwise might not be addressed, or addressed in time.
- Rural Indians use their phones to keep in touch with migrant family members and friends, for securing information on healthcare and education, and for

economic purposes such as learning information on agriculture, employment, trading, and credit.

- Many people in rural areas use their mobile phones only to receive calls from their migrant family members or others: A missed call is a signal to the receiver. That way they are not charged for the call.

~~~

We see Sigamani's expression change, just slightly, after he puts the drums away. He is more subdued again; the light has left his eyes. Now he is back to being the genial, humble host.

He leads us from the Saami room to the living room, where his wife smiles at us as she stands, ready to wait on us or answer any questions we might have.

Simply to make conversation with her, we ask her how old she is.

She shrugs and smiles. "Who remembers all that? Nobody retains records of these things."

In many cultures, a woman does not like to divulge her age. In rural India, most women could not tell you their age if they wanted to. It is more common for someone in rural India to say, "I am around forty or forty-five." That is probably the age of Sigamani and his wife, give or take.

Continuing the conversation with her, I ask where she was born.

"I was born in a small farming village," she replies. "The distance from here is rupees four [six cents] in bus fare."

Rupees four. A new measure of distance. Not in kilometers, but in bus fare. That measurement makes the most sense to her.

After all, if she doesn't have the bus fare to get someplace, who cares how far it is?

Sigamani: "Aside From Children, What Else Is There?"

She tells us that she takes the bus weekly to Utheramerur to buy vegetables, and occasionally goes there to the free government medical facility as well. For one hour a week, an extension clinic of an NGO operates out of their own village.

The tour of the house does not take long. Besides the living room and the Saami room, there is a bedroom for the younger daughter, and a kitchen.

Though we do not ask, we surmise that Sigamani and his wife sleep in the living room on the floor.

~~~

Neither Sigamani nor his wife went to school. Instead, Sigamani was trained in the way of his family. He comes from a family of barbers, and has been giving haircuts and shaves for more than 20 years. His father, his grandfather, his uncle, and now his son: all barbers. Though when he grew up, he had other plans. As a young man, he went to Chennai and made tents. But his family was frightened for him in such a large city and convinced him to return to the village.

And so he returned, and became a barber. But he says, after a while, he had to leave his village. (Just as age is a vague concept in rural India, so is time. Even when pressed, Sigamani is not certain of the years, and references time in approximations. For him, what's past is past, and therefore fades away; what's to come is not yet here; what's here now is what matters. So, time blurs, like something receding and becoming fuzzy in a car's rearview mirror.)

"Why did you have to move from your village?" we ask.

"Because there are too many barbers there already. Not enough work. My father, my brother, my uncle. They all were barbers in the village. So I moved here. Come," he says, and he shows us a low stone wall about thirty feet from the house. It is where he cuts hair. He gets his

58

customers from people who walk by. Sometimes he would have several people stop; on other days, no one. The village is not big.

Once he came back from Chennai, he says, his father quickly found a bride for him in a neighboring village, and she gave birth to three children in rapid succession.

When he talks of his children, a bit of the light in his eyes returns. "They are good children," he says. "My son is smart. He is a hard worker. He has saved his money and added on to our house."

We begin to walk down the dirt road. He is leading us on a tour of the village.

"When I was young," he says, "I wanted my independence in Chennai. Then I came back and started a family. I started my business. I learned how to play drums. And through it all, we always had food to eat. We never went hungry."

He says this with a bit of pride. And with good reason.

In rural India, it is not easy to survive. Of 193 countries catalogued by the United Nations, India ranks 147th on the list of countries in terms of overall life expectancy at birth (64 years). The United States, by comparison, is ranked 40th with an overall life expectancy of 78 years. (Japan is #1 at almost 83 years.)

And it is not just the number of years, but the quality of those years. Life in rural India is not easy on the body. It has not been easy on either Sigamani's body or his wife's body. The physical toil, coupled with the lack of accessible health care or the ability to pay for it, make people in rural India age quickly.

But they do not complain about their hardships.

The Perils of Life Among the Rural Poor

No one likes to have an accident or injury. But for the rural poor, such an event can be doubly troubling, because the event can be a serious financial hardship for them.

Sigamani: "Aside From Children, What Else Is There?"

For example, in the year previous to this interview, Sigamani injured his foot when he got it caught in the gears of his bike. He received 18 stitches, and his medical treatment cost him Rs. 2500 (about $38 USD). To people with healthy incomes, the amount isn't staggering. To Sigamani, it was a significant loss and cost.

Later in that year, he had severe stomach pain, and called 108 (the equivalent of calling 911 in the US). He waited for two hours but could wait no longer and borrowed a car to take him to a government hospital. Once there, he found another long wait, so he was forced to go to a private hospital to be treated. He spent far more money at the private hospital than he would have at the government hospital, but the pain was severe, the need was immediate, and he had no choice.

Incidents like these can send the rural poor into such a debt that they can never recover.

~~~

Sigamani does not like to talk about his past and in particular about his father, whose mental illness took a toll on the entire family. But he does like to talk about his son, a barber who has set up his shop about five kilometers from Sigamani's house. The son has set up shop wisely, Sigamani says: at a crossroads where much traffic passes. He is eager for me to see his son's shop, so we drive there. Normally, Sigamani says, he either walks to his son's shop, or a driver along the way will stop to give him a ride. His son has a motorbike to get to and from work.

His son's shop is nice indeed. It is well lit and has a long wooden counter with many bottles and containers of barber supplies – lubricants and sprays and gels and dyes and other products, none of which Sigamani used when he barbered. Sigamani stuck to scissors and razors and combs. Underneath the counter are shelves with more products and equipment.

Voices From Subsistence Marketplaces

This appears to be a shop set up for serious business. Sigamani's son has a much grander vision for his shop, for his business, and for his life.

The son greets us with a quick smile. He looks like his father, but the flash in his eyes, the vitality in his movements, signify that he is different from Sigamani. Simply in his intense focus and concentration as he cuts a customer's hair, you can see that he is a young man who is not willing to walk languidly through life. He is a man who harbors great plans for the future, and who will stalk those plans doggedly until they come to fruition.

Sigamani smiles secretively at his son as he watches him work. The pride in Sigamani's eyes is evident.

The son finishes with his customer, combing the customer's hair and letting the customer see the cut in his wide mirror that extends the length of his countertop.

The customer smiles, gets up from his chair, pays for the service, and leaves the shop, allowing us to talk with the son, who tells us that he has had the shop for about two years. He fell into the business, he says, more by default than anything else. "I didn't enjoy studying and I didn't know what to do," he says. "So I decided to set up shop, like my father."

He learned his barbering skills from Sigamani, who would use an earthen pot as a head and train his son to hold scissors to it with a steady hand and imagine cutting hair.

The son's business is just enough to make ends meet. He keeps his shop open from 8:00 a.m. to 8:00 p.m. daily, but most of his business comes on the weekends, when he might give 30 haircuts and 20 shaves. His average monthly income is between Rs. 5,000 and 6,000 (5,000 rupees equals about $73 USD).

So the son has followed in the father's footsteps — but he has grander plans for his business. Because his business is at a bus junction between many villages, he gets a lot of college students. "They watch movies and ask me for things like a facial, a bleaching, or a center spike," he says. "I would like to start a men's beauty parlor soon." His hopes are that young adults would be willing to pay for the extended services that a beauty parlor could offer.

And so the son is following the father, but with plans to exceed his father. Which makes the father happy, because that is what he wants, too.

~~~

As we drive back to Sigamani's house, we are struck by the intergenerational continuity in Sigamani's family. They belong to a barber caste, people who are skilled in medicinal abilities and wisdom. Traditionally, people in this caste would treat patients for various illnesses, assist in childbirth, and cut the hair of their patients—originally to remove the hair from around wounds that needed to be treated. Eventually, from this custom, this caste became the barber caste. The medicinal portion has been largely lost, but the barber tradition is carried on, generation by generation.

But Sigamani's son's grander vision for how he carries out his role and business as a barber also speaks to the intergenerational differences that will crop up in any culture. The son has a new way of carrying out his business, a bigger vision for what his business and his life can be.

We pass a banyan tree, and it reminds us of Sigamani and his son. The tree has some branches that are intertwined, but these branches eventually veer off to the side, going in their own direction.

Just as Sigamani and his son are from the same roots, but the son, while still entwined with his father, has his own direction to pursue.

~~~

On the drive back to Sigamani's house, Sigamani speaks of a changing of the guard in his house. He is retired, though he occasionally helps his son in the shop when his son needs help. It's his son who handles the household finances; they keep their money in a cupboard in the house. His is a day-to-day existence; a question about the future elicits a curious glance; why would he think about the future when the day has enough troubles of its own?

But he does take comfort in one aspect of his life: his children.

"My children are good children," he says. "They have no problems. We raised them and provided food for them." Besides his son and his eldest daughter—the one who is married and living in another village—his youngest daughter works for an apple company.

"And if my children are fine, then it is fine with me," he continues. "I don't want anything else."

"Nothing else?"

"Aside from children, what else is there?" he says.

Gender and Marriage in Rural India

As in many cultures, the welfare and happiness of children is paramount—as is displayed in the almost universal desire for children to find a good spouse. As we talked with Sigamani he addressed his goals for his children.

"I want my son to get married," he said. "Marriage is the supreme goal in life, even more so than education. I want my son to marry and live peacefully."

We asked Sigamani if he has a role in helping his son realize that goal. He immediately nodded and said, "Oh yes. I will begin asking around about suitable girls for his son. If I find one, I will ask non-family members to make sure she is suitable."

Sigamani: "Aside From Children, What Else Is There?"

He explained that once a suitable girl is found for his son, then he would initiate a visit with the girl's family.

As for his married daughter, when we asked about her future, he shrugged and said, "Because my daughter is married, for me it is a case closed."

Sigamani.

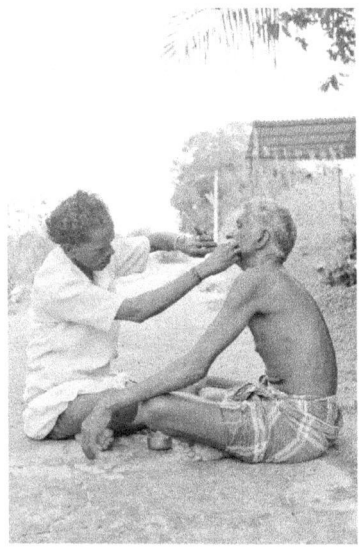

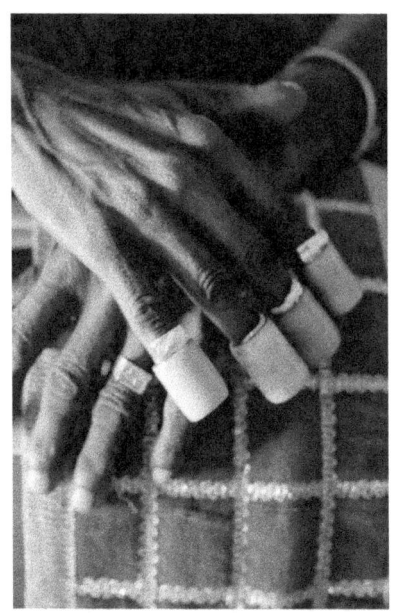

Sigamani giving a haircut
to a neighbor.

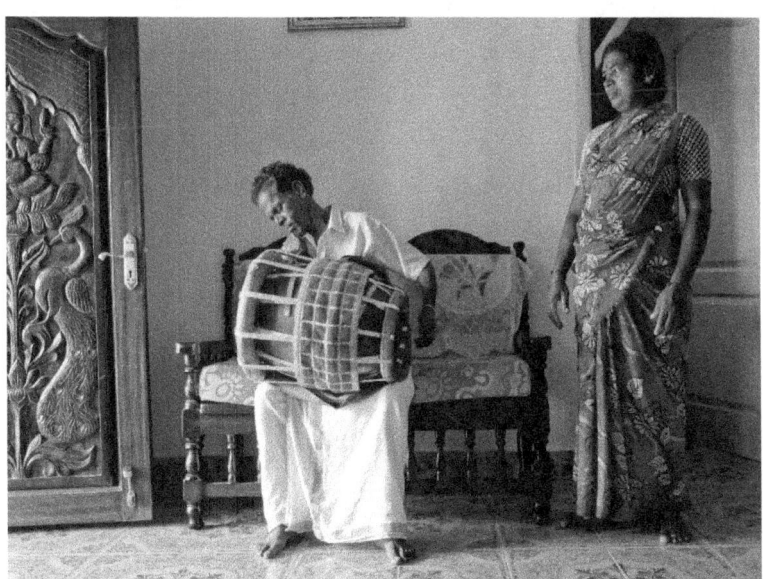

Photos: Alpana Aras | www.alpanaaras.com

Chapter 6

Rani: Strength For The Day

"I knew it was up to me. My children were depending on me. We had rent to pay. So I started going out in the world. I started to meet people. Before I had never gone out on my own."

Rani, who is in her early 40s, sits across from us at a table in an interview room in Chennai in Tamil Nadu, India. She is dressed in a beautiful olive and blue sari—the same sari we saw her in two years earlier, yet she has kept it in pristine condition, looking brand new. She wears two simple maroon bracelets, one on each arm. She is reserved to begin with, and her eyes are guarded, but over the course of an hour, she lets down her guard and shows a wide range of emotions and feelings, ranging from hope to despair to determination to worry to agitation to conviction to regret and back to hope again.

That's a lot to feel and show in an hour, but Rani has been through a lot, and each day takes an enormous amount of strength for her to face.

We will let her tell her story in her own words.

~~~

I was born in Meenambakkam [near the Chennai International Airport]. That is my mother's place. I now live in Kodambakkam [about 12 kilometers north of Meenambakkam]. I am married but my husband has abandoned me. He is a drunkard. He works occasionally as a decorator for weddings; he never brings the money home. He uses it to buy alcohol. He is worthless to me, worthless to my family.

The Impact of Alcoholism in a Patriarchal Society

The abuse of alcohol, and in particular alcoholism, can tear families and lives apart in any circumstance, rich or poor. But it has a devastating effect on individuals and families living in subsistence, because the line between surviving and sinking in subsistence is already very thin, and having an alcoholic in the family dramatically tilts the odds against that family. Families in subsistence rely on every family member to help out, to contribute, in some way to their financial and emotional health and wellbeing. Alcoholism in subsistence conditions seriously impedes a family's hopes and chances for advancement.

In addition, living in a patriarchal society also has an impact on those living in subsistence, and when combined with alcoholism, the impact is magnified. For example, if the husband is an alcoholic, his capacity to earn income is likely going to be negatively affected. He will be out of work or be able to gain only irregular work (and will often spend what he makes on alcohol). But because of the mindset acquired through growing up in a patriarchal society, this same alcoholic husband will typically frown upon, try to dissuade, or simply demand that his wife not work outside the home, because, to him, it brings him shame. And so the women with alcoholic husbands find themselves in very dire straits, with little money and with generally little encouragement from their husbands to earn money.

Such a situation turns difficult situations into nearly impossible situations. Yet we have encountered many women, like Rani, who handle such situations with incredible grace and strength. Some women, like Padmavati (the subject of a different chapter), have husbands who are supportive of their wives working outside the home, but most women do not receive such support.

I have two sons. They are good boys. But I feel so bad, you see. They are 23 and 21, but they had to quit their education early. My oldest son finished sixth grade only; my younger son finished eighth grade. They had to help with augmenting the household income, because my husband never brought any money home. And now he is gone. He left our home in a rage because my sons were arguing with him about his drinking, about his not bringing money home. He went to live with his mother. He should have been a help to us, but he was not. He was a burden to us, one more thing we had to worry about, one more thing we had to take care of. His burden has been heavy all these years.

The Stigma of Divorce in Hinduism

Hindu civil code permits divorce, but the religious code, as such, disapproves of divorce. Marriage is seen as a sacred bond that should be broken for no reason. Traditionally speaking, there is no concept of divorce in Hinduism. Marriage is a sacrament, sanctified in the presence of gods, and is a commitment that is seen as extending beyond this life, up to several generations. So to divorce would be a great sacrilege, and particularly so for a woman.

Those who are divorced find it difficult to be accepted among their friends and family and to find new partners. Because of tradition, because of social, cultural and religious norms, most women stay in a marriage, however hard and difficult that marriage might be.

There is change and progress over time, particularly among middle and upper classes of society. But at the subsistence level, the traditions relating to marriage and divorce are much slower to change.

But my sons are not like him. They are hard workers. They understand the need to work. My oldest son is an electrician, but his work is sometimes on, sometimes off. My youngest son has work as a glass cutter.

She stops, looks down, wrings her hands. When she looks up, her eyes are moist and troubled.

They still live with me. I don't know what I would do without them. My oldest son, he gives me Rs. 5000 per month, and my youngest son, he gives Rs. 4000 per month. You see why I say they are good boys. But if we had had money when they were younger, they could have stayed in school. They could have a brighter future.

Even so, I will tell you one thing. They will not be like their father. They are not like him at all. And for that I am happy. For that I am very happy.

She looks at us to see if we understand. We do. We then ask her to describe her day. But her mind is elsewhere; her eyes flash with anger as she recalls her past.

I should have known better. My own father was an alcoholic. He did very little work, too. And the burden came to my mother, and to the children. My husband was kind to me before we were married. He hid his drinking. It did not seem like a big thing. But when we were married he started drinking as often as he had money to buy alcohol. He no longer cared. He had me to take care of him. I was more like a nurse and caretaker to him than a wife. A lot of people drink because they are afraid. They drink to forget their troubles. But they only cause more troubles for other people.

For some time, I had a steady job. I worked as a cook in the home of a family who had a nice house. I took a bus every day to their house, I made meals for them, and I did a little house cleaning too. Then I would take the bus back home. That was when my sons were just beginning school. I would make them food to eat and then I would make a dinner for us. I cooked all day long.

69

Padmavathy: Happy, Healthy, and Wise

My husband would ask me for money for alcohol when I got home. I would tell him no. He would threaten me because he was the man and I was the woman. I had no right to keep all the money, he said. The money was ours together, he said. I told him I was not going to work all day so he could drink and then what would we do for our rent and for food and for the education of the boys? He would grumble and I would have to go outside because I was so angry at him. And I would think of my mother arguing in the same way with my father and I would start to cry. It would not be so bad if my husband worked regularly, but he never did. He worked only when his thirst was greater than his laziness.

So I worked as a cook for that family for a few years, but then they moved away and I had no work. I was very upset. I didn't know what to do. Even my husband stopped yelling at me because he saw how upset I was. But still he did not get regular work. Still he was not so concerned that he helped out.

I knew it was up to me. My children were depending on me. We had rent to pay. So I started going out in the world. I started to meet people. Before I had never gone out on my own. Other than working in that family's home as a cook, I had stayed at home. But after they moved, I met some women and borrowed money from a chit fund. I decided to start my own business selling flowers. I borrowed money for a cart and for the flowers. I had to buy flowers each morning and, by the end of the day, if they did not sell, they were no good any more. So I would have to throw them out because no one would buy them the next day.

I did not know what else to do. I had to make money. Some days I would sell all my flowers. I would not make a lot of money, but I would make a little. Some days I would have to throw many flowers out. And at night I would cry in bed. I would cry quietly so no one would hear. In my heart I was panicking; I was anguished. I did not know what would become of me or my sons. I told myself I cannot keep buying flowers. I do not make much money even when I sell them, and overall I am losing much money.

Risk Born of Necessity

Rani's situation evokes a common theme among women in subsistence contexts: She had no money and, in her case, a husband who was no help financially or in any other way. She was forced to stretch beyond her comfort zone and push out into the "great unknown"—a world in which she would need all her wits to create an income for her children and herself on which to live. It is hardships such as this that push Indian women living in subsistence beyond their homes and into the working world—though most often with little or no education or job experience.

That is where Marketplace Literacy Communities attempts to fills a void in a small way, by providing the education that women need to function effectively in the marketplace.

~~~

So I looked for a different job. My husband, at these times, he would go off on his own. He would be gone for days or weeks at a time. He was of no help at all. The only good thing he ever did was give me my two sons.

I found a job in a canteen, cleaning utensils and pots. The work was not every day, but when I did work I got paid. I did not have to worry about that. I knew I would get paid, unlike when I bought flowers to sell.

I made enough to pay the rent, barely. By this time my sons had started working and they helped out too. But the canteen was not steady work. I needed more work. I needed steady income. So I kept looking.

71

Padmavathy: Happy, Healthy, and Wise

I joined a self-help group. There, I got the idea for a clothing business. So I borrowed more money to start the business. I buy saris and blouses and nighties at wholesale and I sell them. And so I have my own business.

She has a look of pride in her eyes, but it is mixed with sorrow and weariness. We learn that she ran a chit fund where she lost money, and the loan she received from moneylenders has put her deep in debt. As she talks about this debt, the look of pride vanishes and she fights back tears. We give her some water, make small talk, and allow her to collect herself. We volunteer to cut short the interview, but she says she wants to go on. So we ask her something simple: to describe her day.

I get up at 7 a.m. I take a bath, and then I cook for the day. Then from 8 a.m. until noon I sell saris. Then on some days I go to the canteen until 3 p.m. On those days I come back and take a one-hour break. Then I work in a house, cooking and cleaning, until 7 p.m. Then I work late in the night selling saris. Then I go to bed.

I have my clothing business, and sometimes the canteen, and I cook for two or three houses. That is what I do all day long, and I do not take a day off. I never stop. I cannot.

She breaks down and cries; tears roll down her cheeks. She cries for a minute and then she composes herself, wiping away her tears, but the sadness in her eyes remains. She sighs deeply. With the inhalation, she seems to gain some strength, some resolve.

I make about Rs. 300 to 350 a day (about $4.50 to $5.25 USD). To make sales is not easy. I have learned to be outgoing; before, I was not like that. I have learned how to talk to people. I have learned many things. I am stronger now without my husband. That is one of the things I learned. I am better off.

We ask her about her sons. She smiles, but her eyes are sad and tinged with worry and regret.

They are hard workers. But without the education, they will live in poverty the rest of their lives. I just want them to be happy. That is my only hope, that they be happy.

She hesitates, pondering something, biting her lip, and then speaks, an urgency in her voice, which trembles with emotion.

Can you help my son? If possible, can you help him set up a glass design business? He is such a hard worker and we would return the money. He is always giving me money, saying "Mom, don't worry, I will give you money."

I will repay the loan if you can only help us out. I want to always repay any loan. I don't want to cheat people. We would repay it as soon as possible. I have no other family to help, no brothers or sisters. Or if possible maybe you could help my other son get a job? I want my sons to settle down. We thank God for what we have. We would pay you back as soon as possible. Can you help, please?

~~~

Rani's plea at the end breaks our hearts. She has sacrificed her whole life to help her sons, with no help — in fact, with negative influence — from her husband. She is in large debt — 2 lakhs, or Rs. 200,000. (This is about $3,000 USD, which is an absolute fortune to someone like her. If she cannot pay the loan back — which surely she will not be able to — the moneylenders will hound her entire family for the money.) People in Rani's situation have very limited sources of loans; self-help groups may not give out consumption loans, and formal sector banks will not give people loans without a credit history. So they must appeal to moneylenders for such loans as Rani's, and the goodwill of moneylenders has strict bounds.

For people in Rani's situation, the need to try out new things is immediate and urgent, and the ability to take a loss such as she did is minimal. Such a loss is devastating and crippling. But for these people, severe risks may have to be taken, and not all of them turn out well. Sometimes the reality is that their situation goes from bad to worse. There is a transformative potential in running a business, but as with all business propositions, risk is involved, and when the business goes sour, people in subsistence may not recover.

In Rani's case, she knows her chit fund and her borrowing have dug for her a deep, deep hole—one that she sees no way out of, but she wants her sons not to fall in the same hole. She would like to provide a better future for her two sons, but her most dire need is strength for the day.

Rani.

Chapter 7

Padmavathy: Happy, Healthy, And Wise

Family is of utmost importance to Padmavathy. "I am proud to have created value for at least two generations," she says. She lives out her values, which include no cheating, no lying, and no borrowing, and she lives out the wisdom gained through hardship, a wisdom that she is passing down to the two generations below her.

Padmavathy is an anomaly. She has lived a life of subsistence in South India for 60 years, in a setting where steady jobs are scarce and careers are all but unheard of.

Yet Padmavathy was steadily employed for 36 years. And in those 36 years, she worked a total of two jobs.

In truth, she has had not two jobs, but two *careers* — one for 16 years selling tea, coffee, and food items from a stall run out of her home in a small village in Tamil Nadu, India, followed by 20 years working in a hospital in Chennai as a housekeeper and cleaner.

And through her steady work, she raised three sons, all of whom live and work in Chennai. One is a driver for a hospital, one runs his own rickshaw service, and one works in the stock exchange market.

"Our sons helped us sell the tea when they were young," she says, referring to herself and her husband, who is four years older than she. We are talking in an office in Chennai, with a big fan blowing cool air on us. "But when they got older, they had to concentrate on their studies. And we were not making enough money. So we moved to Chennai in hopes of making more money." Padmavathy was born in Chennai and married when she was 20. She and her husband moved to the village where he had grown up, Arichampalai. The village, with about 450 residents, is about 150 kilometers south of Chennai. She and her husband rented a small house and they bought teas and later on coffee and small perishables that they sold from a stall outside their home. It provided a meager living, barely enough to get by on.

"But the boys were good," she says. "They saw our struggles. They did not ask us for things beyond our economic situation. They were supportive."

Padmavathy has not lived an easy life. The physical and mental stress of making ends meet through physical labor should have taken a harder toll on her body than it appears. She moves with a quiet grace; she is composed and peaceful; and she has the firm skin and smooth complexion of someone 30 years younger. Indeed, when you ask her about her health, she says "It is God's gift. I don't have diabetes, no high blood pressure, which is common after fifty years. I don't have any problems. I am healthy." She beams proudly as she says this; she is proud of her good health.

When Padmavathy and her family moved to Chennai a little more than 20 years ago, she looked for work that would provide steadier income than her tea stall. She found what she was looking for in a hospital job. For 20 years she worked in her steady, quiet, efficient way. She made Rs. 12000 a month (about $174 USD). When she retired, she received nearly four lakhs of rupees (400,000 rupees, or about $5,827 USD). Part of that retirement money came from her own contributions made to an Employee Provident Fund; the money she put in was matched by her employer. In addition, she receives a monthly pension of Rs. 2000 (about $29 USD).

Padmavathy and her husband never made a lot of money, but what they made they used wisely. "We did not stretch ourselves beyond our means," she says. "We did not spend foolishly."

Padmavathy: Happy, Healthy, and Wise

Padmavathy also picked up insights from her business dealings with her customers. She has a network of customers who act as a major source of information for her. "There are good people and there are bad people," she says. "I can tell who the good people are, and I learn from them."

From one, she learned early on about the value of saving, and how to do so in a chit fund (a fund generated from within a self-help group of about 20 women, who can borrow from the fund with small interest). From another customer she learned about the wisdom of investing in land. It is not often that you use the terms "subsistence living" and "investing in land" in referring to the same person. But Padmavathy is not your typical person.

So she and her husband invested in land. And after many years, they sold that land, and with that money they bought homes for each of their three sons.

"We provided them a start," she says. "And that makes me happy."

Padmavathy has found happiness and contentment through her work experiences and her family life. She remembers each work situation with fondness.

"The tea shop helped me bring up my children, because at that time they were very young," she says. "I could work at home and take care of them too. And I take satisfaction in running a business that provides nourishment to others. It is good to feed others."

The hospital provided steady work and greater income. "It helped in educating the children, and in providing for their marriage," she says.

And now she is retired—at least from the hospital. But partly so as not to be a burden to her sons, and partly perhaps because her body is so used to working, she found a part-time job in a canteen in an industrial complex in Chennai. There she works "only" four hours a day, five days a week, setting out food trays, exchanging the money for the food, and cleaning up afterward. She gets Rs. 200 ($3 USD) per day for her work. Each morning she rises at 4 a.m. (which is sleeping in for her, as she used to rise at 2 a.m. to fetch water from the village water tank). Early in the morning she blesses her home and creates a colorful chalk design outside the home. She walks her grandchildren to school and returns home to take a nap before going to her job in the canteen. But she finds time to keep her home in pristine condition. It is both clean and everything is in its place.

"My sons are supporting us," she says. "But I like to have my own income. I don't like asking for money from others. I don't want to depend on my sons. I want to get the things I need from my own income."

There is one thing she does not mind taking from her sons, however: the pleasure of spending time with her six grandchildren. Talking of them brings a big smile to her face.

"I was happy in the village," she says. "Then when we migrated to Chennai, I did the hospital job, and that was good for us. And now through my sons, I have three grandsons and three granddaughters.

"I am very happy with my grandchildren."

Family is of utmost importance to Padmavathy. "I am proud to have created value for at least two generations," she says. She lives out her values, which include no cheating, no lying, and no borrowing, and she lives out the wisdom gained through hardship, a wisdom that she is passing down to the two generations below her.

During a discussion involving Padmavathy and one of her granddaughters, who was in 9th grade at the time, the two compared their lives. Padmavathy grew up in hardship with six siblings in a home where their father died young. In contrast, her granddaughter has few material goods, but she has a father and no pressing hardship.

"My life is easier," the granddaughter says. "I have just one brother, and we get to watch TV." She watches the Comedy Channel, a music channel, and a cartoon channel—on a flat screen TV, a very aspirational product—and she occasionally gets to watch a movie. She has also read all the Harry Potter books (in both English and Tamil) and enjoys reading books. These are luxuries Padmavathy never dreamed of as a young girl.

"I want to be an accountant," the granddaughter declares proudly, with an expectant air of one who can see no reason why this would not happen.

Padmavathy smiles at this declaration. "I just want her to study hard and lead a virtuous life," she says.

You can see, too, the differences between generation when you ask them if they ever dream of traveling. The granddaughter pipes up, "I want to go to theme parks in the USA, like Disneyland!" As for Padmavathy, she simply wants to go to temple; she is very grateful to God for taking care of her and her family.

But she has not lived a life without dreams. "My dream was to get my sons married," she says. "I was not able to educate them much. If I had educated them they would have grown higher. I wanted them to have their own house, to own a business, and to get married."

They do own their own house, thanks to Padmavathy and her husband, and they are married (her daughters-in-law are all part of her extended family) and gainfully employed. One daughter-in-law is a teacher.

"My other daughter-in-laws are going for jobs," she says. You can see she is proud of her sons and of their families. Family means everything to her, and in her family there is a perceptible feeling of being upwardly mobile.

Padmavathy spent six decades living in subsistence, and about four decades working steadily at a few jobs to provide for her family. She rose each morning to meet with equanimity the challenges of the day. She was driven and guided by a simple but powerful goal: to feed her family and herself. Doing so, she says, satisfies God's will for her.

Though she is happy, though she is healthy, though she has been guided by wisdom throughout her life, she hopes for a better future for her family.

"My daughters-in-law should not face struggles like I did," she says. "They should not come across that struggle. They should live happily."

Madhu and John (authors) with Padmavathy and her neighbors.

Padmavathy's granddaughter
showing us their kitchen.

Alpana Aras | www.alpanaaras.com

Photo: Alpana Aras | www.alpanaaras.com

Photo: Alpana Aras | www.alpanaaras.com

Chapter 8

Kamala: Regaining Her Jewels

"Even though everyone struggles, relatives in the village do not respect those without money or jewels," she says. "That is the nature of people in villages." And so her daughter went 10 years without seeing Kamala's parents. Left unsaid, one senses a pride in Kamala that did not allow her to take her daughter to her parents' village without those jewels. It would be, in her eyes, admitting that she was not succeeding as a mother.

Kamala's smile lights up her apartment as she welcomes us in. The floors throughout are all wood, scuffed and worn but clean and polished. She gives us a tour of her apartment: In her kitchen are a table, three chairs, a stove, and a shelf on a wall that holds jars, crocks, plates, and a few knickknacks. Her living room has sparse furniture but is bright and clean. If this were your only foray into India, you would suspect that dust is outlawed. Her bedroom has a small dresser and a bed that is made up with a light multicolored blanket over it. The bed is made with military sharpness. Daylight from large windows floods the entire apartment. We return to her living room and she ushers us to two chairs. We sit and she sits opposite us, still smiling, a charming blend of enthusiasm, affection, hospitality, warmth, and intensity. You sense this is a woman who knows what she wants and goes after it.

She offers us tea, but we politely decline. We have been warned to drink only bottled water while in India.

Not Lacking in Hospitality

The dozens of people that we have visited over the years—many of whom have received us in their humble apartments or huts, some with dirt floors and not a stick of furniture—are uniformly warm, welcoming, and gracious. While most are sorely lacking in fundamental resources, they are all rich in the gift of hospitality. They draw or paint elaborate, time-consuming welcome signs for us; they draw beautiful pictures with various colors of rice powder on the cement in front of their doors; they offer us whatever they have in their house: tea, biscuits, the best chair (if indeed they have chairs) in their home. They dote on us and patiently answer all of our questions, and they receive us as if we were heads of state.

Such hospitality immediately breaks down whatever barriers (socioeconomic, geographic, racial and ethnic, cultural, on and on) that might exist between us and unites us. We feel more like long-lost family being welcomed home than we do inquisitive foreigners intruding in their lives.

It is humbling and enriching for us to witness and be the subjects of such grace and hospitality.

~~~

My eyes wander to a small table, where I see a stack of schoolbooks.

"Are those your books?" one of us asks.

"No, they are my daughter's," she says, beaming. "She is in college."

That raises an eyebrow. Most people we have talked to from her community have stopped their education somewhere between 5th and 8th grades. Kamala herself was forced to stop at 8th grade. She wanted to go on and still now, at age 44, harbors faint hopes of continuing her education—but now is not a good time, because she is too busy.

She bursts with pride over her daughter, who is in her first year of working toward her BCA (Bachelor of Computer Applications) at a college in Chennai, in Tamil Nadu. The degree covers three years, and it is possible, with a government loan, that her daughter might go on for her master's degree and possibly even a PhD—or at least that is what Kamala hopes. Her daughter, she says, plans to be a lecturer in college.

"In life we have crossed many hurdles," she says of her husband, her daughter, and herself. "I have learned many things. People do not respect you if you do not have money. So we want to earn more money. And I want my daughter to live a good life. I want her to be highly educated beyond our status. In spite of earning low income, I want her to study well."

That is one wish that Kamala has got. Her daughter is now in college, the crown jewel of her life.

~~~

In India, jewelry holds great significance, even for the poorest of the poor. In fact, among the very poor, jewelry is utterly desired, because it is linked with wealth, power, and status. Females receive jewelry as gifts at birth, at coming of age, in marriage, in becoming a mother, and on other special occasions. Jewelry not only accentuates beauty; it offers a bit of insurance, because one can pawn the jewelry, if the financial need is great enough. But it has to be a matter of eating or not eating for most women to sell their jewelry.

When Kamala was young, she had beautiful gold jewelry—necklaces, bracelets, and earrings. She entered into an arranged marriage at age 25, and not long into her marriage she had to pawn all of her jewelry—30 sovereigns of gold—because her husband's shop was doing poorly.

"His shop was not in a good location," she says. "His parents backed him for that shop to make him more appealing as a marriage match, but they did not consider the location. We lost much money and had to move to a new location." That move, their debt, and their food and living expenses were all paid for by selling her jewels, which she mourned.

Kamala grew up in a village about 500 kilometers south of Chennai. She was born into a caste associated with doing business; her father was a shopkeeper, and she pitched in with her mother and brother to help at the shop. (When asked how many castes there are in India, she laughs. "Numerous," she says. "I should say countless." Castes, she explains, are grouped in clusters. The upper class is a cluster; so are the Brahmins, who perform *puja* (acts of worship) and prayer in the temples. Another cluster is the MBC—Most Backward Class—which has 108 castes, and the OBC—Other Backward Classes. There are Scheduled castes and Scheduled Tribe castes as well. "Castes are social and communal," Kamala says. "You can change your religion to Christianity, Hindu, or Muslim, but your caste will never change.")

While her family did not have a lot of money when she was growing up, they did not struggle as she did when she got married. Within a year of her wedding, her husband had lost his shop, she had given birth to her daughter, and they had moved to a better location for a new shop—which was doomed to failure after several years. During that time, they lived hand to mouth, were unable to pay rent for stretches at a time, and borrowed money from her husband's sister. To supplement their meager income, Kamala and her husband started a wastepaper recycling business, collecting used paper and selling it for Rs. 10-50 per kilogram to wholesale dealers. It was a lot of work for very little money, and it was a dark time not just financially, but emotionally as well for the normally effervescent Kamala—particularly when she had to sell her jewelry.

"Even though everyone struggles, relatives in the village do not respect those without money or jewels," she says. "That is the nature of people in villages." And so her daughter went 10 years without seeing Kamala's parents. Left unsaid, one senses a pride in Kamala that did not allow her to take her daughter to her parents' village without those jewels. It would be, in her eyes, admitting that she was not succeeding as a mother.

"We did not go to our native place at all," Kamala continues. "My own child did not know her relatives. We stayed where we were. It was only when my child completed fifth standard that my husband took her to their native place for vacation."

Her husband would journey to his native village to get money at times, and would be gone for a month at a time on these journeys. Kamala and her daughter would get by on rice and yogurt, with Kamala waiting anxiously for her husband's return.

When their second shop failed, they moved to another suburb of Chennai where her husband's younger brother was running a milk business. That move was 13 years ago, and it is the last move they have made.

~~~

Nowadays, Kamala says, her husband rises at 3 a.m. to get the milk and water that he delivers each morning. "The wholesale dealer delivers the milk and water to our doorstep," Kamala says. "For the deliveries in our neighborhood, he walks, delivering milk to baskets outside of house doors. For longer distance, we use a two-wheeler." The two-wheeler is a small motorbike; it has a rail on which they can fit five 30-liter cans of mineral water. Milk deliveries come first, though, for two reasons: The milk is chilled, and must be delivered within a few hours, and, perhaps more importantly to their customers, "they need the milk before five or six for their morning coffee and tea."

Coffee is one of those global common denominators, where many people cannot bear to begin their day without their coffee just as they like it.

Kamala rises between five and six a.m. and after her coffee starts her day with cooking and household work. After her daughter leaves to take a bus to her college classes, she helps her husband with the water deliveries. In the afternoon, her husband will return to the houses and businesses he has delivered to and collect money owed.

"We have been delivering milk now for almost 13 years," Kamala says. While she is grateful for the steadiness of this work, she also notes that if the milk spoils by the time they deliver it, their customers will refuse the milk and Kamala and her husband will be stuck with the cost and receive no income. This is, in part, why they picked up additional work.

"Just two months ago we started to deliver the cans of water and also flour," Kamala says. "For the flour we must go to the wholesaler to pick it up."

They pay Rs. 16 for each water can and sell it for Rs. 30. For the flour, they buy a half kilogram for Rs. 9 and sell it for Rs. 10. For milk, the government sets the price; they get only Rs. 1 profit per liter. They got into the water business for the higher profit margin.

A side note about the water is that the government provides it free in this low-income neighborhood. Government trucks bring in water from time to time, and people stand in long lines to get the water. Many times arguments and fights erupt, because the water is scarce. In addition, there is concern about water-borne disease through this free water, which is stored in a common tank, chlorinated, and delivered through pipes;

middle and low-middle class citizens are Kamala's and her husband's water customers.

~~~

Kamala's life is one of hardship mixed with, and overcome by, undying optimism and a relentless determination to improve the lives of her daughter, her husband, and herself. Were the situation different, she would likely be a quite successful entrepreneur, always staying ahead of the game, always extending her boundaries, always envisioning a better, brighter future.

Even in her own financially-strapped situation, she has plans to develop their business, but with her daughter's education expenses, expansion is difficult. "We need one lakh (one hundred thousand) rupees for improving our business," she says, with much of that being for transportation costs of the water. One lakh of rupees equals about $1,456 USD. While they make a gross profit of Rs. 14 for each water can, eight of those rupees are gobbled up by the transportation cost, so the net profit is only Rs. 6 (9 cents) per can.

"We need to improve that," she says. "After paying all the expenses and rent we don't have enough liquid cash." Indeed, they are still paying off debt; it is a slow process with the relatively little income that they make.

When asked what she has learned through her experiences in her business and life, she thinks a moment and then says, "One, location is important in business. Two, no money means no respect. Three, it is good to not be dependent on others. Four, only have the number of children you can support. We stopped at one because we worried that we could not feed another child."

~~~

Kamala and her husband work pretty much from the time they get up to the time they go to bed. They work seven days a week. For relaxation, Kamala watches a few serials on television, and the news; she likes to be informed about what's going on. (Most of those we interviewed who owned a TV were given it for free by the government.) Not long ago, she saw a show that highlighted the 7 Wonders of the World. The list of wonders varies a bit; the Taj Mahal is on some lists.

"I knew only of my village when I was growing up," she says. "I like to learn about different places, different cultures and practices. I would love one day to see the Taj Mahal." The distance from Chennai to Agra, where the Taj Mahal is located, is nearly 2,000 kilometers (nearly 1,250 miles). Yet her daughter, who has just entered the apartment, says with airy confidence, "I will take you not only to Agra, but to see all the wonders of the world." Her daughter has the same bright cheerfulness that her mother possesses, the same energy and half-glass-full optimism. And she has reason to. Her college degree will open up greater opportunities than her mother ever had.

Kamala looks with pride on her daughter. She may have had to give up all of her jewelry many years back, but her daughter is her crown jewel, and her dreams for her daughter—that she be well educated, that she gain a good job, that she not be dependent on anyone—are coming true. Kamala may yearn to see the wonders of the world, but even now, in her apartment, she is content.

"I have worked hard, and so has my husband," she says cheerfully. And, hand extended toward her daughter, she says, "And this is what I have to show for it."

~~~

91

Kamala: Regaining Her Jewels

Kamala bids us farewell at her door, wishing us well and thanking us for coming. Her smile energizes and lifts my spirit. As we walk back to our car, I think of her efforts and perseverance, of her ingenuity and flexible creativity in helping her family stay afloat, in helping keep this resource-starved portion of Chennai, of India, of humanity, afloat. Like the stars in the sky, there are countless Kamalas across the world who form the backbone of subsistence societies, who keep the social fabric together wherever they are.

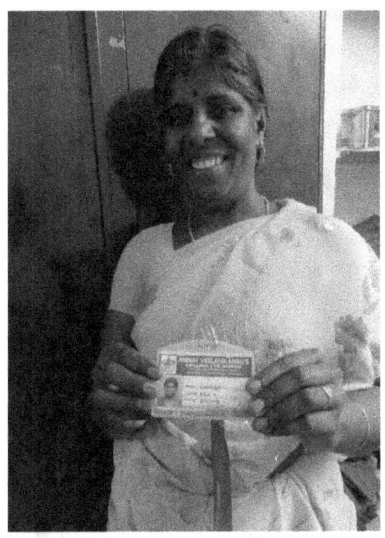 

Kamala proudly show us her
daughter's college I.D.

Kamal in her bedroom.

Top right and bottom photos: Alpana Aras | www.alpanaaras.com

Photo: Alpana Aras | www.alpanaaras.com

Photo: Alpana Aras | www.alpanaaras.com

Chapter 9

Kaniappan:"Circumstances Change, So Must I"

"I did not know who I could trust or what I should move toward," he says. "My uncle tried to help me, but I had to find my way and figure out what I should do with my life." Trust is important in all cultures and strata of society, but never more so than for people living in subsistence, where misguided or misplaced trust can lead to disasters that many can't recover from.

Kaniappan's circumstances, truth be told, were never that great.

He grew up in poverty on a small farm in Tamil Nadu, near Pondicherry, about 150 kilometers south of Chennai. The middle of three sons, he knew the meaning of work on a sheep and goat farm. He and his brothers would help his father mend fences, feed and water the livestock, milk the goats, sheer the sheep, and do whatever else needed to be done.

But Kaniappan also knew the meaning of play. He was imaginative, adventurous, and fun-loving, and always getting his brothers to play with him once their work was finished.

It was this fun-loving, thrill-seeking nature that got him in trouble and forever changed his circumstances.

One early-summer afternoon in 2004, when he was 15, he talked his brothers into going to a telephone pole on the edge of the field that their goats were grazing in. Grinning, he suggested a contest: see who could climb the highest on the pole. His younger brother was not so sure about the idea, but his older brother shrugged and said Sure, why not, and so they climbed.

95

Kaniappan: Circumstances Change, So Must I

The older brother went first, and got about two-thirds of the way up the pole. Kaniappan turned to his younger brother and insisted that he go next, not so much as an act of courtesy, but to see how high he would have to climb to win the contest.

Well, his younger brother did not get as high as his older brother before he wanted to come down. Kaniappan clapped and cheered as his brother descended the pole, partly in encouragement of his brother, and partly because he knew now that he would win the contest.

"I'll show you how to do it!" he said.

He spit on his hands, rubbed them together, gave his brothers a devilish grin, and started to shinny up the pole. It had a bit of tar worn into the wood, helping him to maintain his grip. With effort, he made it halfway up, and then paused a moment, breathing hard.

"Come down!" his older brother called to him.

"No!" he replied, his arms and face glistening with sweat. He nodded upward. "I'm going to beat you!"

Kaniappan resumed climbing. His leg and arm muscles began to ache and quiver with the exertion. His breathing became more labored. Still, he slowly ascended, intent on beating his brother's mark.

Sweat began to sting an eye. He blinked, trying to get the sweat out, but his eye still stung. He stopped, and with his right arm tightly wrapped around the pole, he used his left hand to rub the sweat from his eye.

As he rubbed, his arm slipped on the pole, and he began to lose his balance. Instinctively, he grabbed at the nearest object to his free hand, to steady himself.

The nearest object was a live wire.

He grabbed the wire. Electricity coursed through his body. The jolt knocked him from the pole; he landed on the ground, unconscious.

He woke up in a hospital, which was to be his home for six months.

When he returned home, he did so without the lower part of his left arm. Doctors had to amputate it at the elbow because of the extensive damage done by the current.

The carefree, adventurous boy was carefree and adventurous no longer.

~~~

Now 25, he can still remember the dark nights in the hospital, the nights when he wished he had just died. The nights when he thought about how he could kill himself.

He tells us about those nights as we sit in a small interview room in Chennai. Outside, the skies are blue and the air is warm and humid. We have been talking of other things, and he is animated and friendly, but as he recalls his time in the hospital, he becomes somber.

"I was in great pain," he says. He had severe burns on the hand and arm that were removed. He had nerve and tissue damage from the current passing through his body. And he had severe psychological pain, because life as he knew it was snatched from him, and it would never return.

He was a boy with one arm and, as far as he could see, no prospects.

"In the hospital, all I could think was, I have no life in front of me. Physically my body hurt. Mentally I could not accept that I no longer had a left arm. What could I do on a farm with only one arm? What could I do anywhere with only one arm? I was only fifteen and I felt my life was over."

We ask him what kept him going, and he slowly grins. His eyes sparkle, showing the adventurous boy in him when he does this.

"There were too many people in the hospital who were helping me," he says. "Doctors, nurses, people helping me with my rehabilitation.

Every day they would come around, they would encourage me. Even other patients. And my mother. She stayed by my side the entire time I was in the hospital. It was like they were all willing me to recover, to live a full life."

And so Kaniappan returned home six months after the accident. His family welcomed him back, and were glad to have him home. But he returned a changed young man, and the changes extended through his family.

And none of the changes were easy.

~~~

His two brothers had to quit school and find work to help pay for his medical expenses. Kaniappan himself did not return to school for two years after his release from the hospital.

"The schools in India are not equipped to accommodate students with disabilities," he explains.

There was something more to the decision not to return to school, and we gently probe.

"Well, also, I was fearful of being teased or bullied by the other students," he admits.

He was still adapting to life with one arm, not an easy thing for a teenager, especially one as active as Kaniappan.

But he possesses a strong mind as well as a strong body and will, and so he did not give up on school. He studied for the 10th grade exams, and passed them. Not long after, his brothers encouraged him to move to Chennai, where he could learn a trade, start a new life, and perhaps continue his schooling. Because of his disability, it was obvious that his time on the family farm would not be well spent.

So, at age 20, he underwent another change. He moved to Chennai, to the house of his mother's brother.

"I figured circumstances change, so must I," he explains.

~~~

"Chennai was a real shock to me," he says, his eyes growing large. "It was so big. I was used to wide open spaces outdoors, to more pastureland than people. Now, there are cars and noise and people and big buildings everywhere – buildings that would block out the sky and close you in. It was almost suffocating at first."

The move to the big city was not an easy one. He missed his family. He missed his old way of life on the farm. He missed playing with his brothers. And he was wary of navigating in the alien environment of a city teeming with 9 million people.

"I did not know who I could trust or what I should move toward," he says. "My uncle tried to help me, but I had to find my way and figure out what I should do with my life." Trust is important in all cultures and strata of society, but never more so than for people living in subsistence, where misguided or misplaced trust can lead to disasters that many can't recover from.

While it was true that Chennai would provide him many opportunities, the options were so many and varied and dizzying that he could not settle on a plan. Finally, he decided to return to school to finish his high school degree, but his entrance exam scores resulted in his being admitted only to one school.

And his fears about being bullied because of his disability at his former school were realized at his new school. Here he was, a new kid, mixing with people who had known each other all their lives. From a small farm, far from Chennai. To make matters far worse, he had no left arm.

He was a potential target for bullying on many fronts.

Kaniappan: Circumstances Change, So Must I

He was ridiculed mercilessly by the students. Going to school became a nightmare that he lived out, day after day. The principal, concerned for his wellbeing, finally suggested that he withdraw from school.

The nightmare for Kaniappan continued. He seemed to be on a downhill slide that he could not stop.

He was far from home and family.

Only one school had accepted him, which seriously jolted his confidence. And once there, he was bullied so badly that he felt forced to withdraw from school.

He had no high school degree, no job prospects.

Oh, yes – and he had no left arm.

"I tried not to despair," he says in the interview room. Outside, people are passing by on foot, bicycle, and cart. A child is scolding a dog, chasing after it, trying to capture it. "I knew I had to adapt to my new circumstances. Otherwise, I had nothing. I would have to depend on others, live in poverty at home. I didn't want that."

He turned to his uncle, who made a living delivering newspapers. His uncle got him a job delivering papers as well, in the early morning and again in early afternoon.

It was a start, a step in the right direction. But it was not enough.

"The money was not enough for me to survive on my own," he explains. "So I kept looking for other opportunities."

He found one in a cigarette company that was willing to take a risk on him. He needed to get a bike, and then learn how to ride it with one arm, to sell and deliver cigarettes to small shops in Chennai.

He scraped together enough money to buy a bicycle. And he gained a few scrapes of his own as he learned to ride the bike. After more than a few falls, he learned how to balance himself on two wheels and one arm.

For his efforts, with his scrapes and bruises still healing, he was given a job.

And the long downhill slide slowed, and then stopped. He began to gain some equilibrium in his life.

Kaniappan is a natural salesman, a people person, and he quickly began making 6,000 to 7,000 rupees per month (about $90 to $110 USD).

Along with this jump in income, Kaniappan experienced a surge in confidence. For the first time, he was supporting himself. For the first time, he was making real money. He was not rich. But neither was he dependent on his uncle or anyone else for his survival.

And he was not being bullied for his disability. Indeed, with each passing day, he thought less and less about the loss of his arm. He had become comfortable with it. He compensated wonderfully with his one good arm, with the rest of his body. The loss of his arm was an impediment, yes, but it was now more of a nuisance. It was not a game-breaker that would diminish what he could do with his life.

He smiles as he relates all of this to us. The boyish sheen of excitement, the thrill of adventure, begins to shine through. It is tempered with hard experience, with a growing maturity and a broadened worldview, but it is there.

~~~

By the time he had been in Chennai for five years, he felt settled. He was on his own, supporting himself. He was doing better with one arm than many people did with two. He was completely adjusted to his new circumstances.

And his circumstances changed again. Only, this time, it was a welcome change.

"I was watching the shop of a friend, who had an appointment elsewhere," he explains. "I would do this off and on, when he needed to get away."

It turned out that his friend's wife had a sister. And the sister would occasionally come into the shop.

One day, the sister came into the shop when Kaniappan was tending it. He was immediately taken by her beauty.

"Can I help you?" he asked, his mouth a bit dry.

She smiled shyly, said No, she knew what she wanted, and she picked up some laundry soap and paid for it. As she did, she asked where her brother-in-law was.

"He had an appointment, so I am watching the shop for him. My name is Kaniappan."

She flashed a shy smile, thanked him, and walked off. He wished he had been bold enough to ask her name – he was usually not lacking in confidence. But he hoped he would see her again, and thought he might, as she was his friend's sister-in-law.

"I found myself very drawn to her," he says. "I knew I had to see her again."

He did, within a week, and this time she opened up a bit more. She told him her name: Abhayam, which means *fearless*. He mentioned to her that he was thinking of seeing a movie that had just come out, *Aashiqui 2*. Had she seen it?

"Oh no," she said, shaking her head. "I don't have money for movies."

He grinned. "Would you like to see it?"

"But I cannot afford to go."

"Yes, but I can pay for you."

She hesitated. He could tell she wanted to see the movie. But she didn't want to take advantage of his kindness.

"Please. It will be fun. I want to see it, but I don't want to go alone, so you'll be doing me a favor."

In a moment, a slow smile crept across her face. "Okay," she said. "I'll go with you."

And that was the start of a budding relationship. Abhayam found herself more and more at ease around Kaniappan, because of his easygoing personality and his charm. She liked his outlook on life – that he did not shrink back from it. She liked his confidence, his boldness, his brash ideas.

Kaniappan, for his part, liked her very much as well. "I liked her from the very beginning," he tells us. "But there was one thing we had to get straight."

That, he explains, is the fact that he has no left arm.

"She never mentioned it," he says, "and if I caught her looking at where my arm should be, she would quickly look away."

Not long into their dating life, he confronted her as they walked down a street one evening. He stopped her and turned her toward him.

"Do you notice anything unusual about me?" he said rather pointedly.

She feigned innocence. "No, not really. Except that you are rather tall."

He rolled his eyes. "I am not talking about my height. You know what I am talking about."

She grew quiet, looked almost afraid.

"I need you to say it," he said. "You are pretending nothing is wrong."

"Nothing is wrong," she said in a small voice.

"Nothing is wrong except that you are avoiding the obvious."

She looked at him, her face troubled. "I know you have no left arm."

He took a deep breath, exhaled, and his face softened. "There. That was not so hard now, was it?"

"I did not want to say it."

"Yes, well I needed you to acknowledge it, because the fact that I have no left arm is part of who I am. It is foolish to pretend it isn't. And I will tell you one thing," he said, his face turning suddenly grim. "I will never, ever use the fact that I have only one arm as an excuse for anything. Ever. Do you understand?"

She nodded, a bit frightened at his angry look.

"I am not angry at you. I am just telling you that my arm is not going to hold me back from living the life I want to live. I can work, I can make money. I can support myself and anyone else. I have a good mind, and my body is strong. I will never use my lack of an arm as an excuse. It is the way it is, and I am doing fine without it."

She nodded again, this time looking a bit more relieved.

"I believe you," she said. "I believe all that you say. I just did not want to make you feel bad by mentioning it."

He relaxed and grinned. "Do I look like I feel bad?"

~~~

From spring to summer to fall, they were more and more together and fell more and more in love. In early October, he asked her to marry him, and she excitedly said yes.

"But I want no dowry," he warned her. "I want no exchange of money. I just want you."

Her family was poor, and he did not want to be a problem to them. But from her mother's point of view, money was not the issue. She did not think that Kaniappan was good enough for her daughter.

"Let me find someone else for you," she told Abhayam one evening.

"I don't want anyone else," Abhayam sharply responded.

Her mother started looking anyway, but Abhayam refused every suggestion and offer her mother came up with. Eventually, her mother reconciled herself to the marriage.

For Kaniappan's part, he and his parents had become estranged in the years after he moved to Chennai. It is an issue he does not like to dwell on; perhaps the mental, emotional, and financial strains of the accident and long recovery took its toll. Perhaps his parents' own constant struggle to survive drained all their energy. Whatever the case, neither set of parents blessed the match – but Kaniappan and Abhayam eloped in December 2013, were married in a temple, and began their new life together.

~~~

His new marriage was not the only circumstance that changed at the end of 2013. Kaniappan quit delivering newspapers and cigarettes and opened a shop near his new apartment, which is just around the corner from the shop. The shop is about nine feet by nine feet, and he sells soap, shampoo, cigarettes, newspapers, water, snacks, candy, and other goods.

Sitting at a table in an interview room in a Chennai office, we ask him how the shop is going. He shrugs. His shoulders tell us that the venture could be going better, but his eyes, burning with determination, tell us that he is going to make it work.

"The things I sell, they are available in many other stores on my same street, many of which are more fully stocked," he says. "The competition is fierce."

"So what will you do?"

He does not bat an eye. "I will get up earlier," he says. "I will be open from 4 a.m. to 10 p.m. I will work hard and respect my customers."

And what does Abhayam think of the store?

Kaniappan: Circumstances Change, So Must I

"She is new to the city, you know, like I was five years ago. She is from a small village. So I am teaching her the ways of the city. She helps me in the shop. Sometimes..." he says, and he looks away, "she is not so sure. Sometimes she is afraid. But I tell her we will be all right."

"And will you be all right?"

He looks at us for a moment, and then lets a small smile show.

"I have come through a lot. I have lost my arm. I have lost my way of my early life, lost my family. I gave up rural life for life in the city. I found a way to make money, to support myself – all this with one arm. And now I have my shop, and I am married to the woman I love."

He ponders all this, and then says, "I will be all right, sir."

He rises from his seat, and we do likewise. When we shake hands, his right arm is strong and firm.

Update:

Things have not gone well recently for Kaniappan. His landlord increased the lease terms for his shop by 50 percent and Kaniappan was forced to leave the business. To make matters worse, the landlord refused to give Kaniappan the 1000 Rs. (about $15 USD) he had paid in advance. Kaniappan was cheated but had no way of contesting the landlord.

What we said earlier—about trust being of paramount importance for those living in subsistence and how misplaced trust can prove disastrous—is unfortunately borne out here.

Kaniappan had to close his shop when Abhayam was pregnant and not working. He has returned to selling cigarettes and delivering newspapers, and he has to rely on her family to supplement the food they are able to buy. He rises at 3:30 a.m., picks up and delivers newspapers, comes home at 7:00 a.m. for breakfast, and then from 9:00 a.m. to 3:30 p.m. he delivers cigarettes to stores. After an hour's lunch, he works in the cigarette shop from 4:30 to 9:30 p.m. before going home for dinner and sleeping on his floor mat until 3:30 a.m. when he rises to do it all again.

When we asked him what his ambitions are, his answer was swift and sure: "I want to provide enough for my son to study whatever he wants so he can live a better life than this."

He says this with no rancor or bitterness. It is the hope that keeps him going: to make a better life for his son. It is a refrain we hear over and over and over again in subsistence contexts.

Kaniappan and his wife at their roadside shop.

The authors talking to Kaniappan and his wife about his shop and
customers.

Chapter 10

Punitha: The Teacher

"I teach them how to persevere through challenges. We all have challenges, every day. But as a group we are stronger. We can help each other. It is no good to give up, to lose hope. That only makes things worse.

"And I teach them to be wise with their money. Use the money you make on necessities. After that, save whatever is extra. I tell them with the money I saved, I bought land, we built a house. With the money I saved my children are going to college. It is possible, even here."

Punitha has always been a keen observer. As a young girl, she saw her low-literate mother selling milk every morning to their neighbors; they owned a cow that grazed on the field near their rented house. She saw her father, who was more regular in his consumption of alcohol than in his work as a porter. She saw her older sister, who never attended school, and her brother, who failed 10th grade. She saw how hard it was for her to get to school, by train because there were no nearby schools, and how hard it was to study at home with only a kerosene lamp for illumination, and how hard it was to pursue education with parents who did not value education. She saw the circle of poverty that enveloped her family, and that encompassed those in her neighborhood.

As a young girl, growing up in Kulathur, a village in southern Tamil Nadu, India, she observed all that, and yet, did not despair. Instead, she saw a way out. If not for her, then for her children. And, eventually,

109

for others whose lives she would touch, though she did know it at the time.

~~~

Punitha loved school as a girl. For her, learning was fun. It expanded her world beyond that of milking the cow and doing household chores and helping her mother sell the milk to their neighbors. It hinted at possibilities that most people in her neighborhood never dreamt of. Learning, she believed, would provide her the building blocks to construct a better future for herself and her family.

Despite her parents' ambivalence toward education—her father especially saw no use in it—she completed "plus two" in school, meaning she went through 12th grade, the first in her family to do so. She did not want to stop there; she wanted to go to college to become a teacher, to share her love of learning with others, but her parents said there was no money to continue her education. Indeed, it was struggle enough to complete "plus two"; she was allowed time to study only after finishing all of her household chores. Now, it was time to get married, time to run a household for her husband. When she was 19, her parents arranged a marriage with a man five years older; he was from the same caste.

"My husband, Vijay, is a plumber," Punitha says. "He does not have regular work, but he gets called by civil engineers for jobs." Vijay, like many in both her family and his, is illiterate.

With Vijay's spotty income—he made about 50 rupees a day (about 75 cents US) on the days he did work when they were first married—Punitha looked to add income to their household. She learned how to sew and embroider, and she began sewing clothes for herself and eventually for her daughter (she would give birth to a daughter and a son), and for others in her neighborhood.

110

"My mother taught me to work hard and to never go into debt," Punitha says. "She taught me to save what money I could."

Punitha, ever the learner, lived that lesson out. Over the years, she saved enough money to be able to purchase a bit of land in a suburb of Chennai and then build a small house on the land. Compared to most of the dwellings we have visited over the years in and around Chennai, Punitha's would be the closest to middle class of all of them.

"I don't borrow money from anybody," she says. "This is the lesson my mother taught us. From my childhood days we won't borrow from anybody. We pledge the jewels if we need money. If we have money we will buy jewels since we have a daughter; we will deposit money in the bank. This is normally used for children's education only. I use the money earned by my husband for the household. I save my salary. I used the recurring deposit and other savings only when we were building our house. Otherwise I will save my salary, which I use for my kids' education."

That saving has paid off. The education that she desired for herself, culminating in a teaching degree from a college, did not happen — but it is happening for both her children. Her daughter is in her third and final year of studying for her Bachelor of Computer Applications degree, and her son is in his first year of a five-year physiotherapy program. Both attend colleges in Chennai. Both are making their mother proud. (During our visit, Punitha's daughter sang two songs for us; she also earns money tutoring younger children in mathematics.)

"And if my daughter wants to do postgraduate work, I will help her," she says. "She attends a Chinese school, Soka Ikeda, in Chennai, and she might have the opportunity to work in China after she graduates." Soka Ikeda is an arts and science college for women; Vijay wants their daughter to remain in Chennai, but Punitha just shrugs and says "We will see."

111

~~~

Punitha herself used to fear going out at all, much less entertaining the thought of traveling to a distant land. But she has changed over the years; naturally shy and soft-spoken, she has gained confidence, first through going farther in school than anyone in her family had up to that time, then through learning a trade—sewing and embroidering—and turning that into cash that eventually led to a land and house purchase, and finally through her involvement and rise to leadership roles in NGOs and self-help groups.

"I have been married 20 years," she says. "For the first 10 years I was a housewife. For the last 10 I have worked outside the house. My husband did not want me to work at first. He said I cannot work in a company. But since what I am doing is social work, he said okay."

For the last five years, Punitha has worked as a field coordinator for Marketplace Literacy Communities (MLC), which helps low-income individuals gain marketplace literacy so they can function effectively in the marketplace as customers and entrepreneurs. MLC currently works in various communities in Chennai and also in villages two hours south of the city. The primary mode of learning is through women's self-help groups and a marketplace literacy educational program; MLC serves about 150 self-help groups of about 15 women each.

Punitha first heard about self-help groups while she was doing her tailoring work at home. She joined a group, was invigorated by the support and help she received and the camaraderie she felt, and soon stepped into a leadership role with the group. With her bent for numbers, she became the group's accountant, and also helped individual women with their personal and professional accounts. Along the way, she naturally evolved into what she had always wanted to become: a teacher.

"I teach them tailoring and embroidery," she says. "I also try to teach them important lessons. I encourage them to always work toward independence, not to be dependent on a bad husband. Women have to earn money on their own.

"I also teach them how to persevere through challenges. We all have challenges, every day. But as a group we are stronger. We can help each other. It is no good to give up, to lose hope. That only makes things worse.

"And I teach them to be wise with their money. Use the money you make on necessities. After that, save whatever is extra. I tell them with the money I saved, I bought land, we built a house. With the money I saved, my children are going to college. It is possible, even here."

The fire and energy in her voice is evident. It is easy to see that she is a positive motivator of women, that she sparks hope in them and helps them build better lives for themselves. They see her as a woman of confidence, a woman who has overcome many challenges to rise higher than anyone in her family, a woman who was able to send both of her children to college. To people in better circumstances, that is not so special; to the women of Punitha's self-help group, it is beyond amazing.

~~~

The woman who feared going out, the woman who rued that she could not go to college to become a teacher, now goes out every day, teaching women how to better their lives. As field coordinator for MLC, Punitha interacts with, inspires, encourages, guides, and instructs great numbers of women in and around Chennai on how to be wise consumers and how to start and effectively operate micro-businesses.

"Before this position," she says, "I did not go out. Now I have come to know about the outside world, I have started to understand everything. I have started to interact with many types of people. There are people lower than us in economic status; we should bring them up."

Some people, she says, come to her so burdened with their problems that they want to die. She gently encourages them to take their focus off of themselves and put it on their children, on positive steps they can take to better their lives and their children's lives. "I tell them what will happen to your children if you die? Will they be better off? They will not. They will suffer all the more. In a self-help group, you get support and help. You learn how to start a business, how to manage your money. Even if you make only a little, you have to know how to manage it; even more so. In self-help groups we help them save. And they can borrow money from the group. There is hope. There is always hope."

Punitha is a living example of that hope. She came from extreme poverty. She pushed hard to extend her own education to plus two, and she became the first woman in her family to work outside the home. She saved money and bought land and built a house. She put both of her children through college. She is constantly improving herself, constantly extending her boundaries.

And she is helping others to do the same. She is truly the teacher that she always wanted to be, sharing the life lessons that she has learned with many other women. She is a vital part of the transformation of lives that is taking place in subsistence communities.

A Quiet But Strong Leader

Punitha by nature is a quiet woman, but that does not diminish her leadership abilities that have risen to the fore in the many years that she has been involved with Marketplace Literacy Communities. She is a keen observer of people; she quickly identifies women who need help and then enables them to the best of her ability.

Punitha is a shining example of the many leaders within subsistence communities who work tirelessly to change the system for the better from within. It is leaders like her who create a ripple effect—

starting with her, extending to her group, and spreading from the group into the wider community.

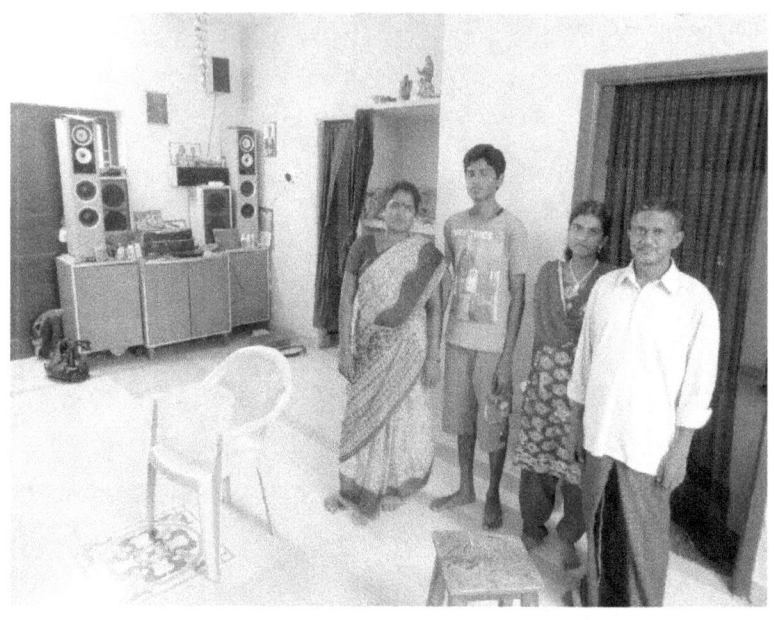

Punitha and her family.

Some of Punitha's embroidery work that she teaches to other women.

Punitha's daughter demonstrates her math knowledge.

Chapter 11

Wisdom Beyond Book Learning

Munusamy saw an even greater opportunity, and, with his usual cordial candor, he pursued a deal that would allow him and his family to live at the mill. In return, he would pay the mill owner a set amount each month, and whatever he made above that amount, he would keep for himself.

It is nearing 6 p.m. in a small village about 80 kilometers south of Chennai, the capital of Tamil Nadu, India. A small but powerfully built man, Munusamy, emerges from his little shop, a ten-foot by ten-foot windowless room that houses two mills, each about the size of a large washing machine. One mill is reserved for chilies and the other he uses for rice and wheat and *ragi*, a cereal grain. He grinds from about 8:30 a.m. to 6 p.m., seven days a week. He wears no watch but the ache in his muscles tells him the time. He starts strong and fresh in the morning, he works steadily through the early hours, sweat pouring from his brow, grinding, grinding, grinding. He works into the afternoon, and the ache in his shoulders and arms starts, but he pushes through the ache. He is drenched in sweat by mid-afternoon, and still he works, as steady as the mill he operates. If there are chilies to grind, he works. If there is rice or wheat or *ragi* to grind, he works. He grinds up to 20 kilos of rice a day, up to 40 kilos of chilies, and up to 20 kilos of *ragi* and wheat. He works into the early evening and the ache in his shoulders and arms becomes stronger, and it goes into his back now too, and he works until his body tells him that is enough for the day, it is time to go home.

And so he makes his way home on his moped, a nine-kilometer ride, first one way down a paved road, then another way down a dirt road toward his neighborhood in the village.

He passes by a neighborhood of small stone and block houses and enters a neighborhood of thatched huts. He continues through this neighborhood of thatched huts, which are all dark because they do not have electricity, and he comes to the only permanent structure in the neighborhood, a house built of cement, a house with electricity.

He parks his moped and enters this sturdy cement house, because it is his, built by his own hands, constructed out of his sweat equity.

He is tired, his muscles still ache, he has a layer of sweat and grime on him, a residue of chili powder and rice powder; he wears his work like a cologne. To him, it is the smell of work, the smell of success.

His wife greets him, and she brings him a bowl of rice. He sits, eats, and watches a bit of television before falling asleep in his chair. His wife gently prods him and he grunts and then rises and plods to bed, where he sleeps a deep sleep.

And during the sleep, the ache in his shoulders and arms and back dissipates, like an early morning fog vanishing in sunshine, and he awakes refreshed, renewed, ready to return to his mill, ready for another day of hard and sweet labor.

~~~

Munusamy takes some time out of an afternoon to talk to some visitors. To give up his work time, time when he can be making money for his family, is a big sacrifice. But he does so willingly, and greets his guests with a warm smile. We sit in a village office building, large and spacious, with high ceilings, and our voices echo a bit. Years of hard labor have chiseled his body into hard muscle.

"I lived in Chennai," Munusamy tells a visitor. "That is where I grew up. I worked in a rice mill, but we had our first child, a daughter, and I did not make enough money at the mill. I made 12 rupees a day there [about 17 cents]. It was too expensive in Chennai." (Now he makes about 12,000 rupees a month, about $175 USD, with a Rs. 5,000 profit each month.)

"So what did you do?" a visitor asks.

He speaks with a directness and a surety that tells you this is a man who is not afraid to make big decisions. And he did indeed make two big decisions that greatly impacted the welfare of his family.

"I moved my family to this village," he says. "I told my wife we cannot afford Chennai because the expenses are too high. They are lower in the village. We chose here because members of my tribe live here."

That move, he says, happened in 2003. He goes on to explain that the work of his tribe in the village was very low-paying. Rice farmers in the region hired his tribe to find snakes in the rice fields and remove the poison from king cobras, blue krait, and Russell's vipers. The venom is used for medicinal purposes.

To most people, such work would be seen as low-paying, unglamorous, and dangerous. But Munusamy saw the work as a temporary fix. The main thing, at the moment, was to relocate to the village. Once that was accomplished, he was confident he could find better work than removing venom from snakes.

Munusamy has only a fifth grade education; after that, he worked to help his family make ends meet. But he has great intelligence and an entrepreneur's heart and mind. And so he knew the move to the village was just the first step. He saw beyond the rice fields, beyond the venomous snakes.

He had worked in a mill, he reasoned. He was a good miller, a hard worker. He had always exceeded expectations of his bosses, even if they didn't show their appreciation with greater pay.

And he knew of a mill in the village. So he visited the mill owner, and offered his services, but the mill owner had no work for him. "But," the mill owner said, "I know someone who might."

And so the mill owner introduced Munusamy to another mill owner. The second mill owner was older, and his body was worn out through several decades of milling. It is hard, grueling and thankless work, and the mill owner was open to the idea of Munusamy working at his mill.

Munusamy saw an even greater opportunity, and, with his usual cordial candor, he pursued a deal that would allow him and his family to live at the mill. In return, he would pay the mill owner a set amount each month, and whatever he made above that amount, he would keep for himself.

"What about repairs and maintenance for the mill?" the owner asked.

"I will take care of all of that," Munusamy replied. "I will pay you the set amount, and I will maintain the mill."

It was a very good deal for the owner. He was happy with the price and he was happy with the arrangement that Munusamy would take care of the machine. It was a no-lose proposition for the owner.

But in Munusamy's eyes, it was a no-lose proposition for him, too. He had gained a place for his family to live. He had found work that he was good at. He had a mill that he was responsible for. His earnings were not limited, beyond what he had to pay the mill owner each month. The more work he got, the more he got paid. He would put aside money each month to take care of any needed repairs. He would not be caught unaware; he would not let his machines break down with no money to fix them.

What he had wrangled for himself and his family was a better living situation. He had the ability to run the mill. Now, in a very real way, he was his own boss, and his work ethic and skills would be better compensated for. His family would also be safer in this small village. He had become master of his own destiny.

~~~

We continue our conversation in the village office. He is wearing a light-colored plaid long-sleeved shirt, open at the neck. His dark eyes glisten with energy and strength. Though he is a busy man, he gives the appearance of a man who is willing to sit and talk all day long with us. You get the feeling that whatever he is doing at the moment, he gives his full attention to.

"That was a big risk you took, don't you think, in taking that mill job?" a visitor asks.

"No sir, it was not a risk. I didn't see it that way."

"Why not? You had to pay the owner a set amount each month, and you weren't assured that amount. So you might have ended up working for nothing. And your family could have been thrown out on the street."

Munusamy smiles, and as he does, a warmth fills the room.

"God gave me a healthy body," he says. "He gave me strong limbs to work with. I am not afraid of work."

We had heard rumors that when someone considered an outsider—such as those in Munusamy's tribe, even though they were part of the village—owed money and could not pay, the creditors were not afraid to use violence to extract payment of some kind. We mention this to Munusamy and he shakes his head, as if ridding himself of a few irritating gnats.

"No sir, I did not worry about that. I just went to work every day. I work hard. I have worked hard all my life."

"So how did you get your work? How did you find your clients, the people you mill for?"

"I mill for my neighbors. I mill for the people in my village. They are merchants, house people, farmers. They come to me and give me the work to do."

He shrugs, as if that was all there was to it.

Here was an outsider, a newcomer to the village, one normally relegated to a low and dangerous form of work, who moved his family to a place where he did not have a job or a place to live. And he quickly got a job and a place to live, and the job offered, yes, great risk, but also more potential than any other job he had ever worked.

Munusamy kept his eyes on the potential. Like a sailor at sea, he kept his eyes on the distant shoreline, and he made straight for that shoreline.

"And so you talked to the people and they were willing to try you?"

"Yes, they tried me. They come to me." Then he grins. "So now I work all day long."

He takes us to his small shop. With four people and the mill in the small space, it is crowded. It is also dim. A bare bulb in the center of the room offers the only light. And the odor is rich with the smell of chilies and milled rice.

He demonstrates how the mill works, talking loudly as he does, because the noise from the machine itself is deafening. He works 10-hour days in this little room with his two loud machines in this dim light, wearing no protective gear—and no shirt, which he removes because the heat is stifling and to protect the shirt.

"When I powder chilies, I wear a handkerchief around my nose and mouth," he says. "The dust is very bad." He has chest pains, lung problems from breathing in the chilies. For five or six years he has daily taken a pain medication for a kidney stone.

"It is still there," he says. "It hurts. But I work."

He is happy for the work and proud of how he has provided for his family. He is a successful entrepreneur, one from a low caste, one with a fifth grade education, one who has not let the large and imposing obstacles in his way deter him. He has simply found a way around, over, or through each obstacle, always keeping his eye on that distant shore, always steering toward his goals, the main one being providing for his family.

His daughter has only a fourth grade education; a younger son has an eighth grade education. They both work in the rice and sugar cane fields surrounding the village. His son also helps him at the mill, and is studying to become an electrician, doing some contract work on the side.

As for Munusamy, he keeps on milling. He is like his machine: strong, durable, relentless. He may be illiterate, but he is wise far beyond books. And that wisdom, mixed with his entrepreneurial spirit, his vision, and his willingness to take a risk, has led to a better life for him and his family — a life where he comes home bone-tired each night, but satisfied.

Munusamy is a man of deep faith. He wears holy ash on his forehead every day, and pictures of Hindu deities are prominently displayed in his house. It is this faith that sustains him through his long, hard, hot days.

"One day," Munusamy says, "I would like to own my own mill. I still pay rent for this one. It is my dream to own one. And I have faith, I have belief that I will."

Knowing Munusamy, he will make it happen.

A fresh batch getting ready to be milled.

Munusamy working at his mill.

Munusamy and his wife standing outside their home.

Chapter 12

Krishnaveni: A Mother's Work Never Ends

Life rarely goes as it is supposed to at the subsistence level. A fishbone kills a son. A daughter dies, leaving behind two young children. The daughter's husband flees home and responsibility.

Even in happiness, life is hard. When her daughter married, Krishnaveni and Abhay were forced to sell their home to pay for the wedding. A happy occasion turns into a threat to survival.

Her husband gets up almost soundlessly, but she sleeps lightly, waking often through the night, and she rolls over to watch him wrap his dhoti around his waist and put on his sattai (shirt).

It is pitch dark, well before dawn, 3:30 a.m.

He slips on his sandals and looks over at her. Her eyes have drifted shut but he knows she is awake.

Even in the darkness, she can see that his thick, wavy white hair is mussed. He will comb it out on the bus, she tells herself.

"I'll be back soon," he whispers.

He gives her a small wave as she opens her eyes and nods.

"Go safely," she says.

He nods and he is gone from their tiny apartment in Chennai, down to the street and to a nearby corner to wait for the bus that will take him to the fruit and vegetable wholesale market. In the roll of his dhoti at his waistline, he carries 2000 rupees (about $29 USD). With that money, he will buy garlic and other vegetables and fruits. He will bring the produce back to his street with his wife Krishnaveni, who helps with the other half of the day's purchases. Besides the garlic, they sell potatoes, tomatoes, bananas, papayas, mangoes, onions, chilies, mushrooms, grapes, dates, guava. That, and more. He buys what he finds available at the market, and what looks good.

The idea is to earn a little more than he spends. So he spends 2000 rupees, hoping to earn 2300 rupees (about a $4.40 USD profit).

His workday, which starts with rising at 3:30 a.m., ends at 7 p.m. But he does not think of that now, not as he is on the bus, which bumps along the darkened streets of Chennai. Very few people are on the bus, and those who are, are quiet. Their bodies sway with the movement of the bus. Potholes and turns on the street cause their heads to wobble on their relaxed neck muscles.

His name is Abhay (not his real name), which means fearless. Abhay closes his eyes, lulled into a state between waking and sleeping by the rocking of the bus. He is well named, for he is fearless, fearless of the day, of the future. That, or he is too tired to worry about the future.

Today, it is garlic day for Abhay. Garlic is a big seller for him. He has steady customers and they have steady needs of garlic for their dishes. But on garlic day, when he buys garlic in great quantities, he cannot take the bus home. The odor is pervasive, and bus drivers will not allow him to haul his garlic on their buses.

So on days like today, he hires truck drivers to bring him home. He will sit in the back of the truck, with the garlic. And he will reek of garlic when he returns home.

But to him, garlic is the smell of money. He puts up with the smell, because it turns into food, into rent, for himself, for Krishnaveni, and for their four grandchildren that they are raising on their own.

Grandchildren bring life and joy to a home, yes. But they also bring needs: food, clothes, education.

And so he rises early each morning, and gets his fruit and vegetables, and returns to Krishnaveni, who has risen and fed their grandchildren – ages 14, 13, 12, and 10. They are fed and off to school. Each morning. Krishnaveni and Abhay prepare the produce for sale. His produce, he puts in a bicycle cart. And he pedals off through the streets of Chennai.

Krishnaveni arranges her produce on her own cart, which is on four bicycle-like tires and is about three feet by six feet. On the street outside her home, she sells produce from her cart from 9 a.m. to noon, and from 4 to 6 p.m. Her cart is yellow, wooden, with paint that is chipped in places and rubbed off in other areas through the years of placing produce on and taking produce off.

~~~

Life has not gone as planned for Krishnaveni. She is now 46 years old. She struggles with diabetes and a breathing ailment.

And she has had to cremate two of her own children.

When she was 33, her son died, and three years later, her daughter-in-law died. So she and Abhay took in their two grandchildren.

When she was 44, her daughter died, and the daughter's husband deserted his children. So she and Abhay took in those two grandchildren as well.

She has one more child of her own, a son, but she has little contact with him, because she does not approve of her son's wife. So communication is cut off with her one remaining child, and she and her husband are left to raise four grandchildren.

On a recent visit to Chennai, I talk with her in a small, open-air interview room that is also used by a school.

"Have you always lived in Chennai?" I ask.

"Oh no, sir. I am from a small village. I came to Chennai because my husband got a job in a glass factory."

"And how old were you when you got married?"

"Fifteen."

Life runs hard for the impoverished in India. She has been married for 31 years, and in some ways it must seem double that, with all she has gone through.

She goes on to tell me that the glass factory closed and Abhay started selling vegetables from a tarp spread on the road while she brought in some money by doing domestic work in the homes of others.

"So Abhay has been selling vegetables for around thirty years," I say.

She shrugs. "I do not keep track, sir. I don't know. But a long time." She raises an eyebrow in appreciation. "And he did well enough that we could afford to buy a house for our family."

Indeed, things went well for her family until, when she was 33, her oldest son, who worked in a fish market, was cutting fish. A fishbone penetrated his finger. His finger got infected. And he died.

It's a jolt to the mind to think that something as small as a fishbone cutting a finger could end in death.

Krishnaveni mourned the loss of her son. "He was so young, and with such young children," she says to me, the sorrow still showing in her eyes. She looks off and shakes her head. "And then, three years later, his wife dies. So we became parents to our two grandchildren."

She gives me a look, and in it I read two distinct messages: *That is not how it is supposed to be.* And, *My heart is full of love for my grandchildren.*

~~~

Life rarely goes as it is supposed to at the subsistence level. A fishbone kills a son. A daughter dies with two young children. The daughter's husband flees home and responsibility.

Even in happiness, life is hard. When her daughter married, Krishnaveni and Abhay were forced to sell their home to pay for the wedding. A happy occasion turns into a threat to survival.

And tragedy turns into even bigger life changes.

It is clear that she loves her grandchildren dearly. It is clear that they are blessed to be in the care of their grandparents. It is also clear that the wear and tear of living at the subsistence level, of rising each day to sell vegetables to make a few hundred rupees, to raise her four lively grandchildren, have taken a toll on her.

Coupled with her health problems, she doubtless feels old before her time.

But she does not complain.

And when you ask her about the future, she looks uneasy for a moment and then shifts her thoughts to her grandchildren.

For them, she sees a bright future. When she talks about them, her face lights up.

"What do you hope for them?" I ask.

It is another day, and I have met her this time at her apartment. It is a tiny apartment. There are only a couple of shelves in the cooking area; most of the pots and pans are on the floor. A small television is on a shelf in the cooking area. A five-gallon jug of water sits on a shelf, a spigot at the base ready to dispense the water. We stand facing each other in this area.

"I want them to go through school, sir," she says fervently. "I want them to find their way, their path in life."

The youngest grandchild, 10 years old, enters to get a drink of water. She is spirited, sharp, with striking features for a girl so young.

Krishnaveni beams as her granddaughter leaves the room.

129

"For her, I have the highest hopes," she says. "She is a very good student. Very sharp."

It almost appears that a few years melt off her face as she talks about her granddaughter. But then a thought clouds her mind, and she says, "But I also worry most about her."

"Why is that?"

"Because in this world, men have an easier time finding their path. It's true," she says, though she doesn't need to convince me. "For my grandsons, I tell them to observe their grandfather, see how he goes about his business. They can learn to operate their own business. But for my granddaughter..."

Her voice trails off, and left unsaid are a litany of worries about her granddaughter's future.

Krishnaveni no longer looks younger. The cloud cover of worry and toil has reappeared, worry and toil and burdens unspoken but always carried.

~~~

Abhay is at the large produce market in central Chennai, near the central bus station. A new day has just dawned. The sky is growing lighter in the east by the minute, but the market is shrouded in a light fog that will soon burn off.

Abhay goes from stall to stall, moving among other buyers inspecting the fruits and vegetables, nodding a greeting to the sellers, most of whom he has known for years.

A low murmur of voices lifts into the air, mixing with the stench of the market, which is strong. The fruit and vegetables ripen and spoil quickly in the summer sun, and Abhay has to be especially careful in the early morning hours, when he cannot clearly see the fruit in the dim light of the breaking dawn. The stench is pervasive, so he must go by touch and sight.

He comes to a stall filled with mangoes and papayas. He picks up a few papayas; they are mainly yellow, tinged with green. He squeezes them, and they give just a little. He haggles in a not unfriendly fashion with the fruit seller. He ends up buying three dozen papayas and two dozen mangoes, squeezing them as well to test for ripeness.

For Abhay, each morning brings a tension, because buying overripe fruit or fruit that is good in the morning but spoils by the afternoon – which is very possible in the summertime sun – will result in loss of income for him. He will have given his hard-earned money away for nothing.

And if the fruit and the vegetables are good, even so there is a tension throughout the day, because the competition is fierce on the streets. Street vendors are common, and if you sell fruit or vegetables that are not good to someone, they will not come back. Or even if your fruit and vegetables are good, people might find other vendors who are selling at even cheaper prices. Abhay's and Krishnaveni's margin of profit is razor thin.

~~~

Krishnaveni understands the ups and downs, the risks, the surprises and challenges, of both business and life. She has learned her own business skills by observing Abhay. She has developed a loyal customer base for her produce. She relies on her husband to bring her fresh produce, and on her customers to return to her, so that each day she and her husband can make a little more than they spend.

One morning, as she transfers tomatoes and bananas and onions and mangoes to her cart, preparing to sell, she tells me that last week was a good week for them: They made a little more than usual.

"So what do you do with the money you earn?" I ask.

"What we do not use for food and rent and things such as that, I put in a chit fund."

A chit fund is a savings scheme in which people periodically pay into the fund and then have opportunities to draw out money, at least the amount they put in, and sometimes with interest. Some chit funds are operated by financial institutions, but many are neighborhood-operated. And most of these neighborhood operations are run by women.

"How long have you been selling fruit and vegetables from your cart?" I ask.

She shrugs. "Two years. We need the extra money because of our grandchildren."

With mention of her grandchildren, I see a few worry lines crease her forehead. She sets to her task of arranging the food in her cart. Her hands are dexterous and nimble; she creates a pleasant, colorful display of the tomatoes and bananas and onions and mangoes in swift fashion.

I know what she is thinking; we have discussed her concerns before. Her health is not good. Her grandchildren are young. They need money for education. She was a mother to her children, and now she is a mother to her grandchildren.

It is a race against time, her body and strength against her grandchildren's needs.

She wants to be there for them. Wants to provide for them. Wants to see them grow up and be successful.

So, she stays in the moment. She pushes her cart across the street from her apartment to its usual spot.

And she smiles brightly at two women approaching.

"The mangoes are very good today," she says.

One of the women nods, smiles, and picks up a mango.

Top: Krishnaveni's home.

Right: Krishnaveni at the local school where we conducted a number of interviews.

Krishnaveni sweeping away the dirt from under her cart.

Chapter 13

Venkat: Relationships Create Opportunity

"It was not easy in our [200-square-foot, single-room] apartment," [Venkat] says. "We had no electricity until I was fifteen. My father worked as a porter in a train station, but he did not make much money."

R. Venkatesan—Venkat for short—is one of the three men who cofounded Marketplace Literacy Communities (MLC), which serves communities in Tamil Nadu, South India. MLC's hub is Chennai, but the operations stretch as far south as villages two hours south of the city.

The two other cofounders are S. Sudhakar and K. Vijayakumar. The three work tirelessly to educate those living in subsistence in South India.

"We work with about 125 self-help groups of about 15 women in each group," Venkat says. "We help them understand how to operate in the marketplace, how to be wise consumers, how to start microbusinesses. And we provide links to financial institutions and assist them in maintaining their financial records."

Venkat has experience as a social worker, an educator, and a research associate. And he is an ideal person to assist these women, because he comes from the same poor background that they do. He knows the hopelessness they face, the fears that haunt them, the slippery slope their lives are on. One unexpected surprise and their lives can receive a jolt from which many will never recover.

Venkat was immersed in this type of life once, and through fortuitous opportunities that came his way and relationships that he

134

became part of, he emerged from it. And now he spends his days helping others emerge from it as well.

~~~

Venkat was born in 1974 in a single-room, 200-square-foot apartment in Mambalam, a residential and commercial district in the heart of what was then Madras and what is now Chennai. He was the fourth of five children born to his parents, who were from a low caste and whose mother, because of her gender and birth order, was intentionally scarred at birth and is partially blind as a result.

"It was not easy in our apartment," he says. "We had no electricity until I was fifteen. My father worked as a porter in a train station, but he did not make much money."

The family shared a common toilet with 10 other families, and often struggled to have enough food. After third grade, his parents sent him to live with his aunt in Chennai. It was for the best, he says. His father was drinking more and more and they had no money. But a year later, his first break happened in the guise of his new teacher.

"Mr. Selvarasan helped me once I got to fifth grade," Venkat says. "He could see I loved learning. I was his top student."

He was also a barefoot student; he had no shoes or sandals to wear. But that didn't hinder him in his studies. It was his desire to learn, his curiosity about subjects, that set him apart from his peers. Most from as poor of a background as Venkat's have no real vision for their lives; they are consumed with finding food for their bellies and sandals for their feet.

That was not the way with Venkat. He didn't know what he saw, but he imagined better things for himself. Better things than being a train porter and living for more than a decade without electricity and worrying every day about having enough food.

Venkat: Relationships Create Opportunity

That better way, he sensed, was through education. His natural curiosity, his bent for learning, would, he hoped, lead him to a better way of life.

~~~

That smooth road to a better life through education did not pan out for Venkat.

His father died when he was in ninth grade, and he had to quit school so he could find a job to help with finances at home. It was a devastating blow for Venkat, who was excelling in school under Mr. Selvarasan's tutelage while living with his aunt. Hopes for his future were put on hold as he looked for work.

"At that point, I did not really think about the future," Venkat says. "I just knew I had to find a job to help my family."

He found one, delivering newspapers. He would rise at 4 a.m. each morning to deliver papers and bring in money for rent and food for his family.

But after about a year of this, his mind returned to what he could do to build a brighter future for himself. Those hopes had just been put on hold, not abandoned.

He was accepted into a diploma course to learn air conditioning and refrigeration skills. He worked in the mornings and studied for his correspondence course in the afternoons and evenings, with an eye toward being a self-employed air conditioning and refrigeration technician in the near future.

But his near future took another turn for the worse.

Two brothers died – one in an industrial accident, the other in a train accident. These deaths, besides the grief they brought, meant loss of income, and put an even greater burden on Venkat to earn money for his mother and two sisters.

After the death of his brother in the industrial accident, he was forced to drop out of the diploma course to find a second job.

"I felt bad for dropping out, because someone else could have been in my spot in the program," he says.

But he had no choice. So he found a job installing floors, and he worked two jobs for a year. He was 17 at this point, and had no great aspirations other than making money to keep food on his family's table. As much as he loved education, as much as he wanted to better himself, it apparently was not meant to be.

~~~

One day his flooring job took him to an NGO, Guild of Service, in Chennai. While he was prepping a floor before installing laminate flooring at the NGO, he was shocked to see Mr. Selvarasan walk past. His former grade-school teacher noticed him, stopped, and talked to him, catching up on what had happened to him since he left school to go to work.

"How do you like installing floors?" Mr. Selvarasan asked.

"I am glad for the work," Venkat answered.

Mr. Selvarasan smiled. "But you always loved learning, didn't you?"

"Yes, sir. But now I work."

Mr. Selvarasan stared at Venkat for some time, a slight smile on his face. "I have an idea for you," he said at last. "One where you could work while engaging your mind in what you love: learning."

Venkat's eyes came alive at that. "What do you mean?"

"We need help here," said Mr. Selvarasan, who helped out part-time at the NGO. "We need tutors for our after-school program, for one thing. We could use a person like you in many areas. Are you interested?"

"Yes, sir, I am very interested!"

Venkat: Relationships Create Opportunity

And so Venkat took a new job, this one at the Guild of Service, which offered programs centered on health, education, social and family welfare, and disability. Without hesitation, he took a job that paid him less than the flooring job, because he saw opportunity in it. And that opportunity was created by the relationship that he had forged with Mr. Selvarasan years earlier.

It is hard to imagine someone living so close to the edge and having the courage to make that kind of decision – one that, in the immediate, would push him even closer to the edge.

But it was a risk that paid off. After a year, Mr. Selvarasan told Venkat that he wanted him to do one more thing for him.

"I want you to study for the twelfth grade examinations," Mr. Selvarasan said. "You are a good student. Good students should graduate."

And so Venkat studied for the twelfth grade exams, which are India's equivalent to a GED in the US. Mr. Selvarasan arranged Venkat's work time to allow him to attend the required classes in a commerce course.

Venkat, at age 19, after he had lost all hope of continuing his education, took the twelfth grade exams. He had always done well in school, but because he was forced to drop out four years earlier, his math knowledge was not up to par, and he failed that portion of the exams.

But he remained undeterred. He focused on improving his math skills, retook the exams six months later, and passed with ease.

And so, at age 20, Venkat attained the diploma in the education that he so treasured, an education that would open up new opportunities for him to rise up out of poverty – remember, this is a young man who didn't even have sandals to wear in school – and make a better life for himself and for those around him.

~~~

When Venkat was 22, Mr. Selvarasan again helped him obtain work, this time as a community organizer, working for the MGR Charitable Trust, responsible for education programs to improve people's education, generate income, improve health, and gain access to loans. But he was not just handed the job; he went through his first interview process, and came out of it having earned the position after impressing his interviewers.

He came out of the experience elated to have the job, particularly as it would allow him to work in an area dear to his heart: helping people. He had grown up experiencing first-hand the help that people in poverty need, and now he was able to extend that helping hand to others. This gave him deep satisfaction.

But while his job satisfaction was at an all-time high, his salary was not; salaries for nonprofits are very low. Although Venkat's job ratings were the highest possible, he needed to make more money.

So he stopped delivering newspapers and started delivering milk, because he had heard you could make more money that way. He would get up before 2 a.m., seven days a week, and he would deliver milk until 6 a.m. If the milk spoiled before he delivered it – and it can spoil quickly in the oppressive South Indian heat – he took the loss.

~~~

The following year, Venkat was interviewing applicants for teaching positions. One of the positions was awarded to a woman named Amul.

A mere three months after working with his new colleague, he proposed to Amul, who happily said yes. But her family did not share her happiness, because Venkat was from a different caste, one that was not as highly regarded as the caste of Amul's family.

139

Venkat: Relationships Create Opportunity

Venkat, undeterred as ever, went to Amul's older brother to plead his case (her father had died a few years earlier).

"I said I wanted to marry Amul, and I would be a good provider for her, but he did not believe I could provide for her," he says. "So I proposed a two-year waiting period, during which I would save money and become even more settled in my profession."

Amul's brother, perhaps impressed with Venkat's determination, agreed to the proposal.

And so Venkat spent a chaste two years working side by side by the woman he loved. In 1999, at the age of 25, Venkat and Amul were married, in a very unorthodox way, according to Indian custom: Venkat funded the marriage and insisted on no dowry. He did not want Amul's money. He just wanted her. He could, as he told her brother, provide for her.

~~~

Two years later, another relationship created the opportunity of a lifetime for Venkat. In December of 2001, Madhu Viswanathan, a professor in the College of Business at the University of Illinois and director of Marketplace Literacy Project, asked Venkat's project manager at MGR Charitable Trust if he could recommend someone to help him with a research project to take place in India. The manager immediately suggested Venkat.

"I was so impressed with him right from the start," Viswanathan says. "Venkat sat through many interviews with me, interviews I conducted for my research project, and by the end of those interviews, I knew I wanted Venkat to work with me."

Viswanathan filled Venkat in on the project plans, and Venkat began conducting interviews for Madhu.

"He picked everything up swiftly," Viswanathan recalls. "He had never used a computer before. He learned to use email and Word and Excel. Everything that I put in his hands I knew I could trust to be carried out, and carried out well."

The connection between Venkat and Viswanathan was propitious for Venkat, because the NGO he was working for closed its doors on December 31, 2003. On January 1, 2004, Venkat began working for Viswanathan full-time in his newly-formed subsistence marketplaces initiative and marketplace literacy project.

"Venkat is one of the three or four truly transformative people in my life," Viswanathan says. "I've been in a lot of situations where I have seen his character shine forth. He is incredibly honest, he lives to work, he is extraordinarily mature emotionally, he never puts other people down, and he is exceptionally gifted in mobilizing a community. He is very talented."

Take a moment to let that praise settle in. Realize that the praise is coming from a highly-honored, world-renowned university professor. And that the praise is directed to someone who lived most of his youth in a room without electricity, who was shunted off to an aunt because his parents had no money to raise him, who went barefoot to school. Who had to drop out of school at a tender age to support his family. Who never gave up, who looked for the good in the world just as he looked for the good in people, and who found the good in the world in two wise and compassionate benefactors, Mr. Selvarasan and Professor Viswanathan.

~~~

Every life has a story to tell. And every story, be it through a book or a movie or real life, has several turning points.

Three of Venkat's turning points hinge on people:

- Mr. Selvarasan, who saw a bright but impoverished student with great capabilities, and who helped him finish his degree and find work that suited him
- Amul, who brought him love, marriage, and children (they have two kids)
- Madhu Viswanathan, who elevated his status as a working professional, giving Venkat the opportunity to reach his potential in working with and helping people

"It's very easy for someone of Venkat's background to be crushed by life," Viswanathan says. "He was raised in poverty, and with the death of his father and his two brothers, things got worse, not better."

But with each of those turning points, things did get better. He found greater opportunities along the way, and started to make more money. Through his work with the Marketplace Literacy Project, he has moved, Viswanathan says, from subsistence level to at least lower middle class level. That's a jump that most people in poverty don't make.

But it's a jump that Venkat made, thanks to his persistence, his abilities, and his relationships with Selvarasan and with Viswanathan.

And more recently, Venkat completed his bachelor's degree – an advanced degree that people starting at the subsistence level rarely even dream of, much less achieve.

"I don't think I am more proud of anyone earning a degree at any level than Venkat earning a bachelor's degree," Viswanathan says. "He worked against all odds. Before that, he took English classes. He continually looks to improve himself."

~~~

Venkat's work with Viswanathan's Subsistence Marketplaces Initiative and Marketplace Literacy Project (MLP) marked the first time Venkat was able to work one job to support a family. In 2005, after 17

142

years of either 4 a.m. alarms for delivering papers, or 2 a.m. alarms for delivering milk, he quit his milk delivery job to focus on his MLP work.

Not only that, but with a loan from Viswanathan, Venkat was able to purchase a small home—more akin to an apartment.

But it is his, and to own his own dwelling place, coming from his background and facing the struggles he did, is an amazing feat.

But no less amazing than his next accomplishment: becoming a book author. He coauthored, with Viswanathan, *Enabling Consumer and Entrepreneurial Literacy in Subsistence Marketplaces* in 2008. He also coauthored a paper with Viswanathan in the *International Journal of Educational Development*.

Not bad for someone raised in a 200-square foot apartment with no electricity and no books, even if there were electricity to read by.

~~~

Venkat now lives in his home with his mother, his wife, and his two daughters. The house is small but nice and clean. There is one bed; the two daughters share it. Venkat, his wife, and his mother all sleep on the floor near the bed.

His goal for his children: to get them a good education and for them to have good jobs, such as in the Indian Administrative Services or the Indian Foreign Service.

At one point in his life – after his father and two brothers had died and he had to quit school and find work to support his family – Venkat could not afford to look ahead. Now, he can. And because of his skills and persistence, he can look to a brighter future for his children.

And you can bet he will stress that they take their education seriously.

But Venkat has more than book smarts. He has people smarts, an emotional intelligence that helped him stand out to employers along the way.

"He has uncompromising focus and a tremendous EQ," Viswanathan says. "You put him in any situation, and he knows how to manage it. He takes ownership and pride in what he does. He creates value in everything that he does, and he's the heart of what we do in India."

Venkat, Viswanathan says, is the epitome of a leader. Venkat defines a good leader as someone who:

- Can create an effective balance of responsibilities among a team
- Operates with mutual respect for those he manages
- Makes decisions
- Is open to suggestions from the team; is not dictatorial

It is a leadership model he got from Mr. Selvarasan and Professor Madhu, he says. And he adds that the confidence shown in him as a leader, especially by Viswanathan, has played a critical role in his leadership development.

Think about this: if Venkat's parents had a little more money, he would not have been sent to his aunt's, and he would not have met Mr. Selvarasan.

Which means he likely would not have gone back to take his twelfth grade exams. And he would not have found himself to be in position to be recommended to Viswanathan.

But thankfully for Venkat, and for the lives of all he now touches and helps, those relationships did happen, those opportunities did open up, and Venkat is now in a position to help those who, like him, needed help.

Paying It Forward

Venkat has not forgotten where he came from, and he has not forgotten the people who are coming up behind him from the same place of poverty and limited opportunity. With the expansion of the marketplace literacy program, which he so ably co-manages along with Sudha and Viji, he is living out his life's purpose of helping others in subsistence learn skills, start microbusinesses, gain self-esteem, and fashion lives for themselves in which they are working toward self-sufficiency and operate out of hope, not fear or apathy. In short, he is paying it forward — giving others the opportunity that Mr. Selvarasan and Madhu Viswanathan gave him.

I have seen Venkat operate over the years, and he holds his employees strictly accountable for their work to accomplish the goals of the MLC, just as Madhu held him accountable. And just as Venkat learned the importance of relationships in his life, he works hard to build relationships with village leaders, teachers, officials, and villagers in the areas where the MLC is expanding.

For example, one time Venkat contacted a group that provides support for people with prosthetics; he wanted to interview someone for one of Madhu's projects. The group recommended Kaniappan, whose story appears earlier on these pages. Venkat met Kaniappan, talked with him, and stayed in touch with him. He continues to stay in touch to know how Kaniappan is doing; we have interviewed Kaniappan several times over the years. Venkat keeps a mental "rolodex" in his mind of the numerous people he has met over the years who would be good candidates for interviews, for research, for self-help groups, and so on. Even though the demand for the people in his network might be sporadic, he maintains a consistent relationship with them to keep the opportunities alive. He does this not only with MLC projects in mind, but because he has a genuine heart for helping people. He knows that being the lowest of the low financially does not mean that people are not to be valued and respected.

Venkat: Relationships Create Opportunity

Venkat first came to the US several years ago. It was his first time outside of India. He was greeted at O'Hare Airport in Chicago and whisked down to Champaign a few hours south. It was a strange new world for him, because he was used to greeting people and being the genial host and helping us foreigners make valuable connections with the people of Tamil Nadu, and now here he was being treated in that same way.

He was nervous the whole way down to Champaign, because he was to present to students in Professor Viswanathan's class, something he had not done before. He made his presentation, and to his shock, the students warmly applauded at the end.

This greatly encouraged him. He has since undertaken to improve his presentation skills; he is always pressing forward to improve various skills. He has learned how to write training scripts, how to use images and technology in teaching, how to edit his messages to make them more powerful. He has produced Day in the Life videos that are viewed by students in the US and around the world. His command of the English language has greatly improved over the years.

All of this started with an opportunity he was given. He seized it, ran with it, and is not looking back. Instead, he is using it to pay it forward to those around him who are in need.

--John Hedeman

| Madhu and Venkat addressing a group of students. | Venkat talking to the team when they visited his home. |

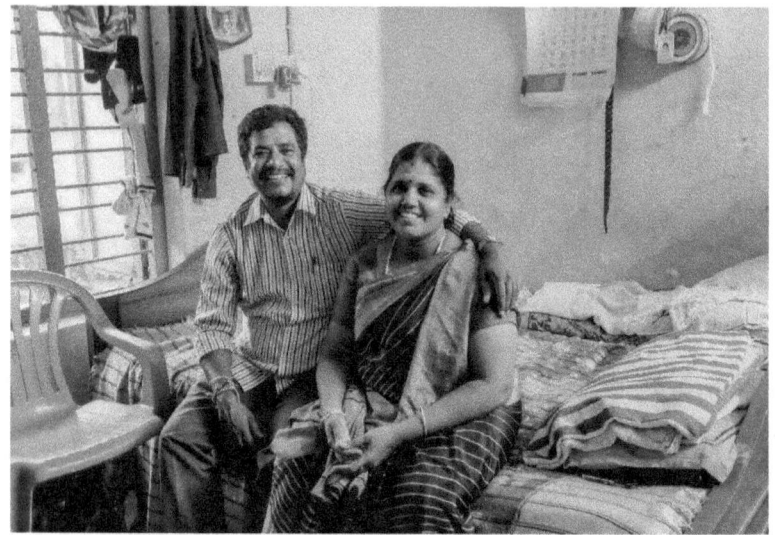

Venkat and his wife in their Chennai home.

Venkat teaching Marketplace Literacy in rural Southern India.

The Team[3]

JOHN HEDEMAN

John is the director of the Business Honors Program and Business Leadership Program at the university of Kansas School of Business. Formerly an assistant dean for the honors at the University of Illinois college of Business, John has been a part of many immersion trips and his ability to connect with individuals in the subsistence setting has led to fruitful conversations within the Voices book.

TOM HANLON

Tom runs his own writing company and has been an essential writer and editor in bringing the *Voices from Subsistence Marketplaces* book to life. He creates content within this collection that simultaneously engages, educates, and motivates his audiences.

[3] We thank Anne McKinney, Coordinator of the Subsistence Marketplaces Initiative, for her assistance in copy editing this book.

SRINIVAS VENUGOPAL

Srini is an Assistant Professor at the University of Vermont. Srini's research examines the intertwined nature of consumption and entrepreneurship in subsistence marketplaces. Prior to his joining the academia, Srini led a technology-based social venture, which focused on delivering educational services to low-income consumers in rural India.

MADHU VISWANATHAN

Madhu is the Diane and Steven N. Miller Centennial Chair Professor in Business at the University of Illinois. His research focuses on marketplace literacy, poverty, and subsistence marketplaces behavior. He is also the founder and direct of the Subsistence Marketplaces Initiative and the Marketplace Literacy Project.

STEVEN MORSE

Steven is a core member of the Marketplace Literacy Outreach team at the University of Illinois. He is responsible for creating the *Voices* web portal and bringing together this book in the format you see here. Steven is also closely connected to MLP's East African Efforts and has begun work on *Voices From Subsistence Marketplaces: East Africa*

S. SUDHAKAR – R. VENKATESAN – K. VIJAYAKUMAR – K. NANDHIVARMAN

Sudhakar, Venkat, Vijayakumar, and Kuppusamy are the field team for the Marketplace Literacy Program in India. Their invaluable assistance has allowed us to recruit the individuals we have interviewed for *Voices From Subsistence Marketplaces*. This talented team has been crucial to spreading the Marketplace Literacy Program to thousands of women in areas of South India and enabling projects like this to be created.

To discover more media and content related to *Voices From Subsistence Marketplaces*, visit us online at http://www.voicesfsm.com/

Voices From Subsistence Marketplaces

www.ingramcontent.com/pod-product-compliance
Lightning Source LLC
Chambersburg PA
CBHW072127280526
45788CB00002B/576